Magickal Crafts

Kristin Madden & Liz Roberts

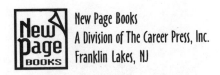

New Page Books
A Division of The Career Press, Inc.
Franklin Lakes, NJ

MAGICKAL CRAFTS
EDITED BY JODI BRANDON
TYPESET BY EILEEN DOW MUNSON
Cover design by Cheryl Cohan Finbow and Marc Roberts
Printed in the U.S.A. by Book-mart Press

To order this title, please call toll-free 1-800-CAREER-1 (NJ and Canada: 201-848-0310) to order using VISA or MasterCard, or for further information on books from Career Press.

The Career Press, Inc., 3 Tice Road, PO Box 687,
Franklin Lakes, NJ 07417
www.careerpress.com
www.newpagebooks.com

Library of Congress Cataloging-in-Publication Data

Madden, Kristin, 1964-
    Magickal crafts / by Kristin Madden and Liz Roberts.
        p. cm.
    Includes bibliographical references and index.
    ISBN 1-56414-839-4 (paper)
        1. Witchcraft. 2. Handicraft—Miscellanea. I. Roberts, Liz. II. Title.

    BF1572.H35M33 2005
    394.2—dc22

                                                        2005053434

For Dave and Karl.
You are my Joy and my Home.

For Marc, Rhianna and Brennan.
You fill my soul with love.

Acknowledgments

We would like to thank everyone at New Page Books for their interest and hard work on this project. Such a beautiful book would not exist without their support and enthusiasm. Both of us are truly appreciative of each and every one of you.

Thank you, the reader, for the celebration and creation you bring to this world. If more of us listened to that inner Muse and created consciously from Spirit, the world would be a much better place. Thank you for all that you contribute. May inspiration bless your every step.

Thank you to Karen and Solange for allowing us to take some of our photos in your lovely gardens. Karen was also a great help in deciding on backgrounds and colors. We are grateful for your wonderful eye for design.

Marc and Dave, thank you so much for your assistance on this book. Marc spent hours cleaning up our photos, and Dave completely rewrote Kristin's write-up of the Mystical Photo Frame, which Dave created in the first place more than a decade ago. You complete us!

Thanks also to our wonderful spiritual and homeschooling communities. Your friendship, encouragement, and support mean more to us than you know.

To our sweat lodge and Peace Pal friends—thank you for sharing in the quest toward a more peaceful world. Together we can change the world.

May peace prevail on Earth.

From Kristin

To my soul-sister and crazy Brit friend, Liz—I have never had so much fun working on a book. My life has been truly blessed since meeting you and I am honored to be your friend.

Dave and Karl, I love you more than words can tell. Thank you for playing with me, helping me, supporting me, and celebrating with me. The two of you have been my inspiration, my instigators, and my partners in this book and all the incredible things we have created as a family. I would not be who I am without you.

Thanks to Mom and Woz for all the fun and wild stuff we explored together. The way I was raised influences my every action and how I see the world. I love you.

The spirit allies that walk with me each moment bless my life and guide me to stay in a joyful, balanced place most of the time (when I listen to them). May my every action honor you.

From Liz

The birds, the trees, the seas...there is so much to be thankful for and so many positive influences to acknowledge when having written a book.

Kristin, thank you for the depth of your friendship. Not many people would see past my dyslexic, muddled brain to the creative writer within and still have the courage to write a book with me. This has been an incredible healing journey for me with lots of fun along the way. Our friendship is like dark rich chocolate to me.

Karl, you are an exceptional young man and the best big brother to Rhianna and Brennan.

Marc, thank you for your constant support and for always believing in me. Thank you for the extensive use of your workshop and all the tools within, not to mention the fact that you have been known to shape wood and edit photos on command. You are my best friend, I am so glad we found each other, I love you, and I love sharing our lives together.

Rhianna and Brennan, you light up my heart, and you are my inspiration. Thank you for just being so amazing and for your enthusiastic help with many of these projects and for letting me work when I needed to. Being your Mum is the most wonderful adventure of all. I absolutely love you guys!

Mum and Dad, thank you for immersing Sue and me in the arms of nature and for letting us play in wonderful squishy mud as kids, but most of all for your love and for always being there for us.

Sister Sue, I am so glad you remember the things I forget and thank you for reminding me.

Carmen, Anita, Dawn, Vickie, Kerry, and Susie-blue, friendship such as ours is not fooled by the separation by space and time because our friendship is a soul sister thing that lives in our hearts. You guys are awesome—you even liked my clay pots when they were all thick and wobbly.

Thank you also to my more recent friends here in New Mexico for your encouragement and faith in the making of this book.

Contents

Chapter 1

Crafting Joy

We love to celebrate. We adore play and creation and parties. Celebration brings joy to life and strengthens the bonds between friends and family. In order to celebrate, you must consciously choose to find the joy and beauty in life. Even when things get rough and you're feeling stressed or wondering how to pay the bills, celebration provides a happy refuge from the daily grind.

For us, the preparation involved in much of our celebrating is about much more than making arts and crafts. It is about opening to creativity and giving voice to our passions, whether through music, poetry, decorating, woodwork, or painting. It is about connecting with and educating our children in a joyful way. It's about creating sacred and inspired homes. It's about refusing to "grow up" and conform to the expected lifestyle of modern America.

Celebration is so good for the soul that sometimes we just celebrate Thursday or the completion of an article or painting or the days our children clean their own rooms. We toast at daily dinners and even say "cheers" with chocolate bars or glasses of orange juice. Sometimes we rave about how beautiful the mountains look at sunset. All of this celebrating really creates a sense of gratitude for even the smallest blessing and a true appreciation for life.

Appreciation is one of the most powerful of magicks. When you honestly appreciate something, you are open to it without judgment. You truly and deeply experience the beauty of its existence and the Divinity inherent in it. This aligns you with the energy of joy and abundance. Allowed to fill your life, that energy builds on itself, attracting people and experiences that resonate with it. Life just gets better and better!

This is what this book is all about. Through offering you a diverse group of ritual tools, sacred objects, crafts, and delicacies, we hope to encourage you to find your own creative spark and apply it to all areas of your life. In this way, each meal can become a celebration and even the smallest decoration can bring joy and magick into your life.

Seeker or Explorer?

Crafting joy is so simple, yet it seems to be so difficult at times. It requires a willingness to put aside any concern about the end result. It demands that you not only fully experience the here and now but that you create the here and now with awareness. We have become a society of seekers, always focused on the goal. Too many believe that if the means don't justify the end, they are unnecessary and unworthy of our time. To live a joyful life, we must be explorers and lovers, savoring every color, every feeling, every taste. Explorers relish the journey and delight in the adventure, simply for the sake of experiencing it. Take a moment to consider if you tend to live your life more as a seeker or as an explorer.

The Explorer's Inquiry

1. What are your plans for tomorrow? Is the entire day scheduled to meet your commitments, or is there room in there for some spontaneity?

2. How likely are you to be spontaneous and try something out just because it might be fun?

3. When you buy a book or consider taking a class, what is your motivation for this? Do you have a specific goal in mind, or do you do it for pure interest and the possibility of fun and growth?

4. Are all your projects devoted to a desired end result? If that result is not achieved, are you able to find pleasure in the process, or is it all just one big failure?

5. When you exercise or go for walks, what motivates you to do this? Are you working toward weight loss or getting in shape, or do you do it just because it makes you feel good?

6. How does your creativity manifest? Do you allow it some freedom of expression, or is it bottled up, always directed toward a goal?

7. When was the last time you played with clay, paints, crayons, or mud? If it has been a while, why is that?

A Joyful Life

Crafting joy and developing an energy of appreciation also demand that you be selfless enough to be selfish for a time. To craft joy and live in a joyful space, even if only for one evening, is a tremendous gift to the world. Consciously experiencing that energy helps us live happier, healthier lives and contributes to that energy around us. It shifts us to a reality where beauty can exist in a cloud, a brightly painted door, or the sparkle of ice on a driveway. Not only is this a fabulous stress-reducer, it creates us as better caretakers, better workers, and just better people to be with. Try a few of these ideas this week and see how it affects your experience of life. You might be surprised to see how much happiness you can find by just spending two minutes, twice each day, on one of these suggestions.

Living in Joy

- Close your eyes, take a deep breath, and be thankful that you are able to breathe. Thank the air, the trees, and the plants for providing this breathable air.
- Walk around your home and feel grateful that you have a place to live.
- When stopped at a red light, look at a weed, tree, bird, or cloud. Feel your connection to this natural object and give thanks that it is here for you now.
- Look around for your favorite color and feel how happy it makes you.
- Tell someone how much you care for him or her and how you appreciate the relationship the two of you share.
- Buy yourself a beautiful flower.
- Cook yourself your favorite meal or get yummy takeout. While eating, focus your full attention on the tastes and textures of the food.
- Fully focus on a pet, if you have one. Pet it or spend time observing it and allow the love you feel to fill you completely. Thank this creature for sharing your life.
- Celebrate Tuesday or Thursday or any day—and do it "just because."

So let's have some fun! We have divided this book in celebratory sections that follow the festivals of the eightfold Wheel of the Year, along with lunar celebrations and some additional holidays that most of us celebrate. This provides a format that encourages creation year-round. It reminds us throughout the year to celebrate and gently guides us away from the tendency to get so caught up in our jobs and our to-do lists that we forget to "smell the roses." Although the contents of each chapter are most definitely not restricted to that section of the Wheel in which they appear, they were chosen specifically because they bring through the energy of that particular celebration in a unique way. So let's talk about that Wheel...

Wheel of Life

The cycle of the year is often referred to as the Wheel of Life. We see life as a circle, connected to all other things. The sacred circle as microcosm of the seasons, the cycles of the day, the phases of the Moon, and the stages of our lives is a nearly universal model among ancient and native peoples. Many of us continue this today in various ways through folk customs and religious celebrations. These are special times, and honoring them as such maintains a regular cycle of joyful energy throughout your personal year.

Wheel of Life

The turning of the wheel follows the circular path of Nature from darkness into light and around again in continuous motion. The Winter Solstice is the darkest night of the year when the Sun is reborn and the light of day begins to increase. As the longest day of the year, the Summer Solstice is the gateway for the return of darkness. The Spring and Autumn Equinoxes are the two times of the year when day and night are of equal length. These four astronomical observances mark the quarter points of the year.

Then there are the four festivals, or sabbats, that come down to us through history bearing Celtic names: Samhain, Imbolc, Beltane, and Lughnasadh. Often perceived as fire festivals, these four intercept the quarter points and were traditionally times of markets and fairs.

These eight festivals are times to rejoice and celebrate the magick in our lives. We are also reminded to look within and contemplate how the flow of cosmic energy affects our own lives and to work with the forces of nature to benefit all.

Personal Wheel

With a little of that magickal creativity you possess, whether you realize it or not, you can create your own small Wheel of Life as a gift or to help remind you and your family of the energies, attributes, and deities associated with each of the eight festivals.

Materials

- 18-inch-wide circle of wood
- ruler
- wood varnish
- pencil
- wood-burning tool

1. Divide your circular piece of wood into 7 concentric circles as follows:
   - Outer ring: ½ inch wide
   - 2nd ring: 1 inch wide
   - 3rd ring: ¼ inch wide
   - 4th ring: 4½ inch wide
   - 5th ring: ¾ inch wide
   - 6th ring: ¾ inch wide

2. Using your ruler, divide the outer ring into 4 equal parts: top to bottom and right to left. Then divide each of these 4 parts into 3 equal parts, creating 12 spaces for the months of the calendar.

3. Calculate the approximate placement of the Winter Solstice (December 21st) and Summer Solstice (June 21st). Using these as a guideline, separate the 2nd ring into 8 equal parts and pencil in the

remaining festivals: Imbolc (February 2nd), Spring Equinox (March 21st), Beltane (May 1st), Lughnasadh (August 1st), Autumn Equinox (September 21st), and Samhain (October 31st).

4. If you associate a particular rune, ogham tree, or other symbol with the seasons or months, add them to the 3rd ring. In the photo, Liz used the ogham trees for her wood-burned Wheel of Life.

5. In the 4th ring, draw the trunk of each seasonal tree at the peak of each season and extend the decorative boughs to the beginning and end of the season. Spring starts with the equinox and is in full bloom at Beltane. Summer starts with the solstice, and midsummer day is at Lughnasadh. Autumn begins with the equinox and peaks with Samhain. The Winter Solstice marks the beginning of winter and Imbolc takes place at midwinter.

6. The 5th ring is for the symbols of the zodiac. The first day of Aries is the first day of spring, so begin the astrological ring in line with the Spring Equinox, then divide the circle in 12 and inscribe the astrological signs in order: ♊, ♋, ♌, ♍, ♎, ♏, ♐, ♑, ♒, ♓, ♈, ♉.

7. On the 6th ring, add planet symbols next to the astrological signs to show the ruling planet of each zodiac sign.

8. Divide the innermost circle in 2 from equinox to equinox. Draw the Sun on the light half of the year (summer) and the Moon on the dark half of the year (winter).

Sacred Space

Many of the sections in each chapter of this book are devoted to sacred space. We offer you a wide variety of altars and altar cloths, tools and oracles, and other "magickal" crafts. Each of these is designed to create an aura of sanctity and spirituality for your rituals and celebrations. But sacred space is much more than the stuff we use to help set the mood and focus our minds and spirits.

Sacred space is special by virtue of the energy we imbue it with and the frame of mind we bring to it. It is sacred because we **believe** it sacred. When we enter sacred space, we feel different. We are inspired, humbled, honored, and filled with love and joy.

Take a moment to imagine the most sacred space you've ever experienced. Perhaps it was a sacred site or a family or group ritual, or maybe you experience Divinity in Nature. Wherever it was, what made it feel so sacred to you? What did you bring to the space that allowed you to feel that energy? What elements of that space do you remember most vividly?

When creating your own sacred space, try to re-create similar elements. Most of us respond best to rich sensory input in order to activate a meditative state and help us open to sacred space. The most powerful rituals involve all the senses.

We have developed crafts that do just that. Incenses and smudge sticks trigger your sense of smell. This is one of the most powerful of our senses and one that stays with us when others fade with age and time. Candles, flags, mobiles, and more all focus your sense of sight. As a visual society, many of us desire beautiful colors and designs for special occasions. Runes, ogham sticks, and clothing are extremely tactile. Rainsticks, rattles, and drums all engage your sense of hearing. And Magickal Delicacies should fully engage your taste, perhaps even your smell and touch.

Honoring Yourself

In offering so many varied crafts, we not only hope to provide you and your friends with years of creative activities, but we also want to honor the fact that not everyone responds to the same things. You may love to create embossed velvet crafts but the idea of gardening is not for you. Or you may just not have the space for a labyrinth or Maypole.

Certainly there is great benefit to be found in working a little bit outside your personal comfort zones, and you may discover a new talent or a new love as a result. But don't feel that you need to do everything to be crafty or creative. You don't! We each have our own strengths and the things we enjoy doing. There is nothing wrong with following your heart in these things. We do. Liz is an incredible potter. She is the queen of embossed velvet and she enjoys using her sewing machine. Although Kristin can sew fairly well if absolutely forced to, her interests lie much more with drums, natural materials such as wood and stone, and cooking. So we go with what we like and are very happy about it.

In crafting joy, we all need to know when is a good time for making new creations and when we just need to take a rest. We understand all too well how sometimes life just doesn't give you enough free time to spend crafting a mosaic firepit or a stone knife. Trust us, there have been times when we wondered if we could schedule a trip to the bathroom or a real meal into our lives. And that is why we made these crafts so diverse.

There are time-intensive crafts in each chapter along with quick and easy ones. There are crafts that are clearly for adults and ones that are specifically for kids. Remember that Kid Stuff can be fun for people of all ages—and when you don't have the time or energy for an "adult" craft, these may be just the right choice for something fun and easy to do. When you just don't feel up to it or honestly can't make the time for a real craft, don't! Pick one of the simple yet yummy Magickal Delicacies and just **relax.**

May your life be filled with joyful magick!

Chapter 2

Samhain

B oo! We all know Samhain (*pron.* SAH-wen or SOW-en) best as Halloween, a time of ghosts and bats and all things dark and scary. It's when we go to fun parties with Otherworldly overtones. Who doesn't remember dressing up as their favorite scary or beautiful or mysterious being? Can you recall the taste of candy corn or the smell of apple cider? We'll bet you still get a kick out of carving pumpkins. We certainly do.

This is a very old celebration that has been known throughout the centuries as a night of the magickal betwixt and between times; Samhain is the time of year when the Veil between the worlds is believed to be the thinnest, allowing communication and visitations from departed loved ones. Traditionally, this time of year is full of history, fun, creativity, and, of course, magick. And it is not just for kids!

Altars and Sacred Space

As a festival of the dark half of the year, Samhain has long been considered a fire festival. Because nights are longer at this time of year, the heat and light of fire are welcome blessings. A sacred firepit and an altar crafted through burning are the perfect additions to any Samhain celebration.

Wood-Burned Footstool Altar

A wooden footstool makes a perfect little altar. Wood burning is a nice way to decorate wood without hiding its natural beauty. For a fire festival, it also brings through the energy of fire in a safe way. On the cover of this book, just under Kristin's name, is a simple yet elegant footstool altar placed outside among the ivy. These unique altars have a natural, simple beauty that is a great choice indoors or out.

Materials

- wood-burning tool
- sandpaper
- tracing paper
- pencil
- varnish or wood sealer
- unvarnished wooden footstool

1. Remove any stickers on the stool and sand any rough spots.
2. Lightly sketch or trace your chosen design onto the stool with pencil.
3. Select one of the wood-burning tool tips. Use a pointed tip for details and a thicker tip for shading and wider lines.
4. Turn on your wood-burning tool and give it time to heat up. Read the manufacturer's directions and carefully observe all safety precautions.
5. Moving smoothly and steadily across the surface of the stool, lightly trace your pencil sketch with the tip of your wood-burning tool. The heat from your wood-burning tool should singe the wood and turn it a mid-dark brown color. If the wood turns black and starts to smoke, work a little lighter and faster. If you see no color change, try working more slowly and pressing more firmly across the wood.
6. Retrace lines as necessary. Then turn off your wood-burning tool and let it cool.
7. If necessary, change the tip and repeat steps 5 and 6.
8. Finish it off with some varnish or a coat of wood sealer.

Mosaic Firepit

Fire was important to our ancestors for warmth and light, especially during the long dark of fall and winter. It is for these, and other, reasons that Samhain has been called a fire festival. Building your own fire pit, then covering the walls with a mosaic of river rock, is a splendid way to honor the spirits of fire while enhancing your own magickal space.

Materials for Firepit Walls

- rubber mallet
- shovel
- two 50-pound bags of sand
- seven 80-pound bags of ready-mix cement
- fifty-four 12-foot wooden stakes
- 20 feet of 10-inch wide aluminum flashing
- work gloves
- duct tape
- knife
- tape measure
- water and hose

1. Select a flat area for your firepit well away from overhanging branches and at least 10 feet away from buildings or property lines.

2. Wearing work gloves to protect your hands, cut the aluminum flashing into 2 strips: one 12 feet long and one 8 feet long. The edges of aluminum can cut just as a knife can, so always remember to protect your hands.

3. Clear a flat circle of bare soil at least 4 feet in diameter. Spread an even layer of sand on top of this circle. Then dampen the sand with a light spray of water.

4. Curl the 12-foot strip of aluminum flashing into a circle. Overlap the ends by 6 inches and tape both ends with duct tape.

5. Curl the 8-foot strip of aluminum flashing into a circle. Overlap the ends by 6 inches and tape both ends with duct tape.

6. Place the smaller circle directly in the center of the large circle on the prepared bed of sand.

7. Once you are satisfied with the placement of the two rings, gently tap each circle ½ inch down into the bed of sand with a rubber mallet.

8. Support the outside wall of the large circle with 33 wooden stakes placed at 4-foot intervals. Support the innermost wall of the small circle with 21 stakes placed at 4-foot intervals.

9. Read the manufacturer's instructions carefully before mixing the cement. It takes approximately seven 80-pound bags of ready-mix cement to fill the donut-shaped walls of the firepit. Unless you have access to a large cement mixer, you should mix one bag at a time. Then distribute the cement evenly around the form before mixing the next bag of cement.

10. Leave the finished form to dry for 1 or 2 days before removing the stakes. Cut the duct tape, then carefully unravel the aluminum flashing.

Materials for River Rock Mosaic

- river rocks
- water resistant cement-based tile mortar
- trowel
- lint-free cloth

1. Play around with the rocks and come up with a simple, attractive design before setting your river rocks permanently in mortar.
2. Mix the mortar according to the manufacturer's directions.
3. Starting at the bottom outer edge, use a trowel to spread a thick layer of mortar over a small section of the firepit.
4. Push each river rock about halfway into the mortar. Continue working around the bottom edge, one section at a time. Then work your way up and over the top of the firepit.
5. Finish off at the inside of the top rim by blending the mortar smoothly into the cement wall of the firepit. Do **not** mosaic the inside of the firepit.
6. Use a damp lint-free cloth to wipe any excess mortar off the protruding river rocks.
7. Do not light a fire in the pit until the mortar has cured for 48 hours.

Tools and Oracles

Have you ever seen a Halloween display that did not include a witch? Sadly, they are usually the scary, ugly, fantasy witches (none of the witches we know has green skin), but the image of the witch flying on her broomstick is a common one at this time of year. And it is no surprise, because this is the time when our spirits fly easily between worlds. It is truly a time of seeing into the realms of shadow—both outside of us and within our own hearts and minds.

Besom

It doesn't get much more Halloween than this. The besom, or broom, is the classical witch's tool. Besoms have a long association with fertility, and many loving couples jump over a broom on their handfasting day. Use your magickal besom for sweeping away negative energy or preparing space for a circle. Keep your besom by the fireplace to ward off unfriendly spirits or lay it under your bed and kindle a little magick in the bedroom.

Materials

- measuring tape
- sandpaper
- optional: wood-burning tool, knife, or paint
- bucket of water
- straight tree branch or dowel: 1-inch diameter
- string
- brush material: grasses, reeds, herbs, broom, and straw

1. Measure the distance from the ground to your chest and cut the branch or dowel to that length.

2. Smooth out any rough spots along the shaft of the branch and round off the ends with sandpaper.

3. Use a wood-burning tool, knife, or paint to decorate the besom handle with magickal symbols or words.

4. To cleanse the brush and ready it for magickal work, soak the material in a bucket of water overnight when the Moon is full. Shake the excess moisture from the brush. Then lay the strands alongside each other with all the tips facing in the same direction and the ends in line.

5. Take a handful of brush and line the bottom ends up 3 inches from the bottom of the handle. Space the brush evenly around the handle and tightly tie it in place with a length of string tied 1 inch up from the bottom ends of the brush.

6. Tightly tie several more layers of brush over the first until you are happy with the fullness of the brush.

7. Bend the top layer of brush (the long ends) over the tied ends so that the tips of the brush now point downward and cover the 3-inch end. Tightly tie the bent brush in place with string just below the first set of ties. Bend and tie each layer of brush until your besom is finished.

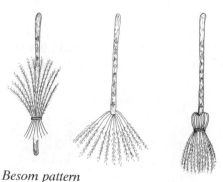

Besom pattern

Scrying Bowl

Seeing into the shadows is made easier at the dark time of the year when the gates between worlds are slightly ajar. But having a tool to aid your spiritual exploration does make things much easier. The scrying bowl has been around seemingly forever. It uses the reflective and emotional qualities of water to focus your attention and allow you to see into the hidden places: the future, relationships, the other worlds, and your own inner self.

Materials

- block of clay, approx. 5" × 5"
- black acrylic paint
- paintbrush
- small bowl of water

1. Knead your clay so that it is warm and moves easily in your hands. Roll it into a large ball then push it down into a slightly flat ball, about 2 to 3 inches tall.

2. Push into the center of the ball with your thumb. Using both thumbs, pinch it into a bowl shape, pushing outward to thin the sides and create a bowl. Be careful not to thin the bottom too much. Wet your fingers periodically to keep the clay malleable.

3. Pull off any excess or smooth the thicker parts into thinner areas. Patch up any cracks by wetting a small piece of excess clay and smoothing it into the crack.

4. When your bowl is approximately 6 inches wide and 2 inches tall, or whatever size you prefer, wet your fingers again and smooth the inside of the bowl completely.

5. Allow the clay to dry completely according to the manufacturer's directions.

6. Paint the inner surface of the bowl black, using at least two coats of paint. You may decorate the outside with symbols or keep it all black. Allow the paint to dry completely before use.

Scrying for Wisdom

To create special water for scrying, allow a glass of water to sit outside under a complete Moon cycle, dark Moon to dark Moon.

Fill your scrying bowl at least halfway with water. Pass first your left hand, then your right hand over the surface of the water, aligning your energy with that of the water. If you have a specific question or situation you want insight into, hold that in your mind as you chant:

> *Blessed water, open the way,*
> *Bless me with clear vision this day.*
> *Clear all blocks, my mind set free,*
> *Guide me now and let me see.*

Keep in mind that you may not "see" anything. Be aware of any thoughts, feelings, or memories that come to mind. Allow them to pass you by so your mind does not wander, but if the same ones keep coming up, give them your attention to determine if they are bringing you a message.

When you are finished, give thanks to the water and to your spirit guides. Dispose of the water with respect and gratitude, either in a garden or as an offering to the spirits of your home.

Crafts

At this time of other worldly contact, many people turn their minds to departed loved ones. We honor those who have passed over and attempt to let them know we have not forgotten them. But because this is the beginning of the cold, dark times in many areas of the world, we also begin to think of staying safe and warm. Therefore, the crafts we offer you in this chapter often focus on protection magick, ancestors, and divination.

Power Pouch Necklace

Adorned with gem beads and a fancy button, this crystal-filled leather necklace makes a powerful charm for attracting good fortune, health, wealth, or protection. One of ours can be found in the bottom right corner of the cover of this book. With a little research and play, you will find the perfect combination of beads and stones for you. See Chapter 8 for a list of magickal stones. A nice healing pouch can be made by sewing the seven colors of the chakras (see Chapter 7) onto the pouch with beads, or you might personalize a birthday pouch with birthstones (see Chapter 11).

Materials

- cardstock paper
- pencil
- leather (1 foot square; 2 or 3 ounce weight)
- leather cord
- scissors
- fancy button
- waxed thread or other thread suitable for sewing leather
- crystal or gem beads
- leather sewing needle or sharp pointed darning needle
- small crystals or gems

1. Copy and cut out the pouch pattern on card stock paper. Trace around the paper template on the suede side of the leather.

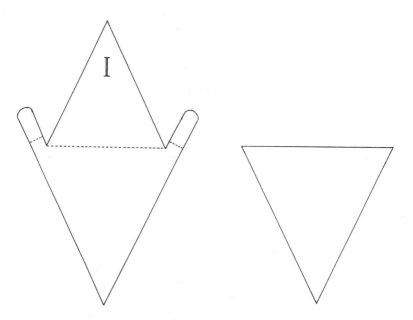

Power pouch pattern

2. Cut the pouch pieces from the leather using a pair of sharp scissors.
3. Sew the button onto the center of the triangle pouch piece.
4. With suede sides together, place the triangle piece of leather on the bottom half of the diamond piece so that the sides line up perfectly.

5. Fold the small left strap into a loop. Sew it in place on the top left corner of the triangle. Continue sewing the front and back of the pocket together along the left side of the triangle. Leave a few extra inches of thread at the bottom of the pouch for tying off and threading beads.

6. Repeat Step 5 on the right side of the pocket. Tie off the ends and thread a few small crystal beads on each long thread.

7. Cut a buttonhole in the top flap to fit the button. Sew more beads on the front pouch if you wish.

8. Thread a length of leather cord through the pocket loops and attach with a knot on each side to make a necklace.

9. Place magickal stones in pouch.

Hold the finished pouch in your hands. Sit comfortably and relax with your eyes closed. Visualize the pouch floating in a clear shallow stream cleansed by soothing water. In your mind's eye, you pick up the pouch and hang it from the branch of an old oak tree. The pouch swings gently in the warm summer breeze. When the pouch is dry, you hold it in your hands and sit beneath the tree. Take three slow, deep breaths and open your eyes in this world. Your pouch is now cleansed and ready to wear.

Squash Lantern

The tradition of carving vegetable lanterns into spooky glowing heads originates from the Celtic belief that the head represents the very soul of a person and holds great spiritual power. Severed heads of heroes and enemies alike were believed to hold the power to ward off unfriendly spirits and predict approaching enemies, thereby giving protection to the living. This Samhain, welcome friends and bring protection to your home with a row of glowing heads.

Traditional lantern heads were made from turnips but you can also use a potato, beetroot, squash, gourd, or even a melon for a unique, protective, and fun lantern. Root vegetables such as potatoes and turnips have firm flesh on the inside and a thin skin on the outside. This combination is a little different to hollow out than the thick-skinned, seed-centered pumpkin squash. For best results, make these little lanterns on the day you intend to use them.

Materials

• a firm round root vegetable, at least the size of tennis ball	• 20-gauge wire
• knife or pumpkin-carving tool	• spoon
	• tea light
• linoleum-cutting tool	• bamboo cane, 3–4 feet long

---

1. Slice off the top of the root vegetable and cut a circle down into the vegetable body, leaving a ¼-inch wall around the outer edge. The bottom of the lantern should be about 1 inch thick and fairly flat on the inside.

2. Cut numerous crisscross lines from one side of the cut circle to the other. Spoon out the hashed center.

3. Cut out the eyes, nose, and mouth with a knife or pumpkin-carving tool. To give your lantern hair and eyebrows, use a linoleum-cutting tool or other small gauging tool to draw shallow detail lines in the outer skin of the lantern. Candlelight will shine through these shallow lines, so you need not cut through the lantern wall.

4. Cut two 6-inch pieces of 20-gauge wire and twist them around the last top inch of a bamboo cane. Leave all 4 ends of wire sticking up 1 inch above the end of the bamboo cane.

5. Plant the unwired end of the bamboo cane firmly in the ground. Choose an open space well away from overhanging branches or anything flammable.

6. Push the bottom of the carved lantern head onto the protruding wire ends. Put a tea light in the center of the lantern.

7. The top of these small lanterns must be left off for the tea light to have enough oxygen to burn. Never leave a burning candle unattended!

Pointy Hats

Inspired by the "Sorting Hat" from the wonderfully magickal Harry Potter books (by J. K. Rowling), this is a fun witchy and wizarding hat with its crooked crown. Check out Liz's son wearing Liz's pointy hat on the cover of this book. This pattern will fit a medium to large adult head. Make a smaller version by cutting the inner circle of the brim pattern a little smaller and shortening the bottom edge of the crown triangle accordingly.

Materials

- roll of brown paper
- 1 yard of 45-inch-wide cotton fabric
- 1 yard of 45-inch-wide lining fabric
- 1 yard of 45-inch-wide iron-on interfacing
- cotton thread the same color as fabric
- roll of 20-gauge galvanized steel wire
- pencil
- pins
- tape measure
- needle
- sewing machine
- string
- scissors
- optional: pliers
- iron
- wire cutters

1. First cut a hat pattern from a roll of brown paper as follows.

   To make the brim, cut out a brim circle according to the size table here. Then cut a center circle from the center of the brim circle.

   To make the crown pattern, draw a triangle. Refer to the table for measurements. One side of the triangle will be the bottom, and the upper two sides will be the associated "crown sides" from the table.

   Before cutting out this crown shape, draw a curved edge at the bottom of this triangle by holding a piece of string at the top point while you hold your pencil at the other end of the string. Using the tension in the string to keep your curve uniform, draw a curved line from one corner of the bottom edge to the other.

Size	Brim Circle	Center Circle	Crown Bottom	Crown Sides
Small	6 inches	18 inches	22 inches	19 inches
Medium	7 inches	19 inches	25 inches	20 inches
Large	8 inches	20 inches	28 inches	21 inches

   Now that you have cut out the brim and crown pattern from paper, use this pattern to cut out one hat and one brim from the fabric, lining, and interfacing.

2. Iron the brim interfacing onto the wrong side of the brim fabric.

3. With right sides together, pin the brim fabric and brim lining together. Then sew a ¼-inch seam around the outer edge of the brim. Turn the brim the right way out.

4. Make a circle of wire the same size as the rim of the brim. Bend a small hook shape at each end of the wire and interlock them to keep the circle together.

5. Place the wire circle inside the hat brim. Then pin it in place snugly against the seam.

6. Sew a second seam around the edge of the brim 1 inch in from the outer edge to enclose the circle of wire. Avoid sewing over the wire, as your needle may break.

7. Iron the crown interfacing to the crown fabric.

8. Sandwich the crown lining and fabric together with right sides together. Sew a ⅛-inch seam along both 20-inch sides. Turn it right-side out.

9. With the lining on the outside, fold the crown in half so that the sewn edges come together on one side. Pin these edges together and sew a ¼-inch seam from top to bottom.

10. Sew a tube for encasing a length of wire by sewing a second seam along the same edge ⅓ inch in from the first seam. Finish the second seam 2 inches from the top point of the crown. Close off the top of this tube with a few stitches.

11. Turn the crown right-side out. Then use the blunt end of a pencil to push the point tip out.

12. Cut a piece of wire 18 inches long. Bend and flatten a small loop at each end. Insert the wire into the tube you just made in the crown.

13. With the right sides of fabric together, pin the brim and crown together. Tack into place with a running stitch. Then sew together with a ½-inch seam. Again, avoid sewing over the wire.

14. Clip the inner edge of the hat brim by cutting out small triangles about 1 inch apart all around the inner circle. Be careful not to snip the seam.

15. Turn the clipped edge toward the hat and cover it with a strip of single-fold bias tape, hand sewn into place.

16. Play around with the hat's shape by bending the wires in both brim rim and crown.

Shrine for the Dead

This petite papier-mâché shrine is a beautiful way to remember the soul of a departed loved one. Not just for departed humans, Liz made one of these shrines when the Maddens' beloved dog, Aiko, passed over. It still sits on the mantle as a beautiful reminder of Aiko, and is a way of honoring her continued place in our hearts.

Materials

- pencil and metal ruler
- corrugated cardboard
- craft knife
- masking tape
- old phone directory or newspaper
- white craft glue
- bowl of water
- clear nail polish
- plastic cloth
- thin Plexiglas
- photo of departed loved one
- small brass hinges with screws
- 6 sheets of scrapbooking paper: 5 for background, 1 for decorative detail

1. Cut out two identical arch shapes, 8 inches wide by 12 inches high, from corrugated cardboard. If you wish, add gentle curves around the top and bottom edges of the arches but be sure to keep the arches identical.

2. Draw an arch-shaped window in the center of one of the arches. This window arch should measure 4½ inches wide by 7 inches high. Use a craft knife to neatly cut out the window arch, taking care to keep the window itself perfectly intact. Trim ¼ inch off all round each door to allow for the thickness of papier-mâché layers.

3. Gently remove the window from the arch and cut it exactly in half lengthwise to form the window doors.

4. Build the side walls of the shrine from 2-inch-wide strips of corrugated cardboard. Use the masking tape to attach the 2-inch strips of cardboard to the rim of the window arch around both the frame of the window and the border of the larger arch.

5. Tape the remaining arch to the back of the shrine with masking tape.

6. Tear up small strips of paper from an old phone directory or newspaper.

7. Protect your work surface with a plastic cloth. Mix glue with water in a 1:1 ratio in a bowl to form the paste. Dip one strip of paper at a time in to the paste and use your fingers to wipe off the excess paste. Stick a smooth, even layer of paper strips all over the shrine, including the window doors. Apply three additional layers of papier-mâché and set all aside to dry.

8. Select some background paper to decorate the inside and outside of the shrine. Rip the paper into 1-inch squares. Cover the shrine with these papier-mâché squares.

9. Cut out small leaves or flowers from a sheet of decorative scrapbooking paper. Adorn the shrine with the cutouts, arranging them over the papier-mâché background. Write a dedication to your departed loved one on the back of the shrine.

10. When the shrine is dry, protect it with a thin coat of clear nail polish.

11. Trim a photograph of your departed loved one to fit inside the arch of the shrine. Cut an arch-shaped piece of thin Plexiglas to fit snugly inside the arch. This plastic arch will hold the photo in place and protect it as a photo frame.

12. Screw the window doors in place with the small brass hinges.

Magickal Delicacies

The final Samhain harvest provides a bounty of delicious foods to enjoy. This is truly the time to savor the last of the fresh corn, apples, pumpkins, and squash. We've chosen two of our all-time favorites to share with you. They are also traditional delicacies in many areas of North America and Europe at this time of year. So enjoy and raise a glass to the blessings of the land as the Earth falls into slumber.

Spiced Apple Cider

Apple cider is a family favorite as the temperatures begin to drop. Children of all ages love to visit apple orchards and watch the apples being pressed to make cider. Autumn apple festivals are great fun for all, full of crisp breezes, warm beverages, and an amazing array of dishes to taste. Adults may want to try a shot of dark, spiced rum added to their cider for a little extra warmth.

Materials

- ½ cup brown sugar
- 1 teaspoon whole allspice
- 1 teaspoon whole cloves
- ¼ teaspoon salt
- 2 dashes nutmeg
- 3 cinnamon sticks
- 2 quarts apple cider
- large saucepan and strainer

1. Combine brown sugar, allspice, cloves, salt, 1 dash nutmeg, cinnamon, and apple cider in a large saucepan.

2. Bring to boiling. Cover and simmer for 20 minutes. Strain to remove spices.

3. Serve piping hot with a dash of nutmeg on top.

Pumpkin Muffins

Close your eyes and imagine the savory smells of pumpkin and cinnamon wafting to you on a crisp, cool breeze. Imagine biting into a warm, soft muffin and finding an explosion of autumn tastes in your mouth. Mmmmm...don't you just love freshly baked muffins? And what better muffins to make at Samhain than pumpkin ones?

Materials

- 4 tablespoons butter
- 1¾ cups all-purpose flour
- ¾ teaspoon salt
- 1 teaspoon mace
- 2 teaspoons double-acting baking powder
- 2 eggs
- ¾ cup cream or milk
- ½ – ¾ cup pumpkin puree
- ½ cup applesauce
- mixing spoon
- small pot
- wire whisk
- 2 mixing bowls: 1 large and 1 medium
- olive oil or butter for greasing pans
- pans for 2 dozen muffins
- optional: ½ cup raisins or cranberries

1. Preheat oven to 400° F and grease muffin pans.

2. In the medium pot, melt the butter over low heat. Do not allow to boil.

3. In the large bowl, combine flour, salt, mace, and baking powder.

4. In the medium bowl, lightly whisk the eggs.

5. When butter is melted, add the cream to the pot and allow to warm slightly.

6. Add butter, cream, and eggs to the flour mixture.

7. Stir gently, leaving small clumps. Do not over-stir. The batter should be thick and sticky.

8. Add pumpkin puree and applesauce. Gently mix in. If you plan to add raisins or berries, do so now and gently fold in.

9. Spoon batter into muffin pans.

10. Bake for approximately 20 minutes, until a knife inserted into center comes out clean.

Traditions From Around the World

In Mexico, Dia de los Muertos (Day of the Dead) is said to be more than 3,500 years old, long pre-dating the arrival of the Spanish conquistadors. As did the ancient Celts, the Aztecs prized skulls. These represented death and rebirth. As such, they were displayed during the ritual to honor the dead, who were believed to return during the month-long ritual. Celebrated today in Mexico as well as parts of Central America and the United States, the celebrations vary by region. Many people wear traditional wooden skull masks and dance to honor departed loved ones. These skull masks are also placed on altars that are dedicated to the dead. You can see our version of an ancestor mask on the cover of this book. Notice how lively and beautiful it is. There is nothing morbid about this celebration!

Ancestor Masks

The Mexican Day of the Dead is a celebration of the circle of life. The skull and skeleton represent the fact that death is part of this natural cycle, just as winter is one season in a year. Painting a skull with bright colors livens up this day and reminds us that it is actually a celebration of life and change. This is a clever and powerful way to honor the ancestors and remind everyone that life and love do indeed continue after the death of the physical body.

Materials

- petroleum or vegetable jelly
- plastic wrap or shower cap
- scissors
- rolls of pre-plastered strips
- towels or newspapers
- bowl of warm water
- paper and pencil
- sandpaper
- craft knife
- pencil
- elastic or ribbon
- gesso or white paint
- black paint
- fine-tipped brush
- optional decorations: markers, acrylic paint, glue, glitter, shiny gems, picture of skull

1. Lay towels or newspapers down on the couch or floor where you will be laying down.

2. Get the pre-plastered strips, scissors, and bowl of warm water ready to go. Cut the strips into sections ranging from 2 to 5 inches long.

3. Liberally cover your entire face with petroleum or vegetable jelly, smearing extra on any facial hair. Cover your hair with a shower cap or a layer of plastic wrap and smear some jelly over your hairline for added protection. Plaster that dries to hair hurts when removed!

4. Dip one strip at a time into the warm water and smooth it onto the area to be cast, rolling off excess water with your fingers as you remove them from the water. Apply 3–4 layers of strips over your entire face, leaving openings for your nostrils.

5. Use additional plastered strips to form the mask into a skull shape. It may help to have a picture of a skull on hand to copy. Ball up or roll strips to exaggerate your eyebrows, cheekbones, and jaws to give the appearance of hollows around the mouth, in the eyes, and in the cheeks.

6. In about 15 minutes, the drying plaster will begin to pull away from your face. Let it dry for at least 5 minutes after completing the final layer before removing. When you are ready, simply stretch and scrunch up your face under the mask as you gently pull it off. It should come off easily if the plaster is dry enough. Allow it to dry for 48 hours before decorating.

7. Use the craft knife to bore two small holes in the eyes for you to see through. Bore two more holes with the blunt end of a pencil on either side of the mask at the temples.

8. Smooth out any rough paper edges with sandpaper. Paint the dry mask with gesso or white paint.

9. Add the skull details with black paint using a fine-tipped brush.

10. Jazz up your skull with some brightly colored paint, glitter, and shiny gems.

11. Thread elastic or ribbon through the temple holes and adjust your mask to fit comfortably.

Kid Stuff

Skeletons and ghosts are just plain fun at this time of year, but kids think about death more than most adults realize. It both intrigues and frightens them for many reasons that vary depending on the age of the child. Children often find it easier to work through fear and other challenging emotions through play and make-believe. Bringing death and change into our lives as normal parts of life, and encouraging kids in fun ways to understand that life and love continue beyond the physical body, are wonderful ways to ease the tension that can surround the subject of death.

Skeleton Puppet

What kid doesn't like puppet shows? Help your kids celebrate the Mexican Day of the Dead and honor their departed loved ones with this unique puppet. It can be hung on a door during trick-or-treating or over an altar during a Samhain ritual. Either way, it is great fun to make and play with. We include a pattern for your use here but to see the finished product, look at the skeleton on the cover.

Materials

- string
- empty cereal box
- tracing paper
- pencil
- knife or scissors
- craft paint: white and black
- craft paintbrush
- fine-tipped paintbrush
- awl or knitting needle
- small round-head brass fasteners
- thin stick of wood or bamboo cane

1. Trace or copy the skeleton puppet pattern.

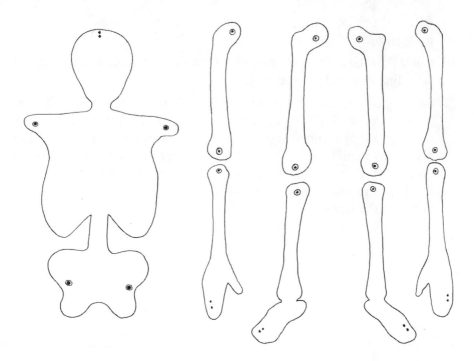

Skeleton puppet pattern

2. Enlarge the skeleton pattern so that the torso/head piece is no larger than one flat side of the cereal box to be used.

3. Transfer the pattern onto the inside walls of an opened-out, empty cereal box.

   (*To open the box, cut along all corners except the front four, leaving a flattened surface.)

4. Cut out all 9 sections from the cereal box.

5. Paint each piece completely white using several coats of paint.

6. Once the white paint is dry, use a fine-tipped paintbrush to paint the skeletal details with black paint.

7. Pierce small holes through the puppet as indicated with an awl or knitting needle.

8. Attach the bones by threading small round-head brass fasteners through the holes.

9. Pierce two small adjacent holes in the palm of each hand, tip of each foot, and top of the head.

10. Cut a thin stick of wood or bamboo cane to about the same length as your finished skeleton puppet.

11. Starting with the head, thread a length of string through the adjacent holes in the skull. Then attach the other end of the string to the center of the wood or bamboo stick. Attach separate lengths of string to the holes in each foot. Adjust these strings to fit perfectly from outstretched toe to stick. Then tie it off at the end of the stick. Connect the hands in the same way but attach the string to the stick halfway between the head and foot string on each side.

Chapter 3

Winter Solstice

For many people, the Yule season really is the most wonderful time of the year. The beauty of lights, savoring warm drinks on cold nights, and thinking about what other people want and need touches nearly all of us. Even those who hate the stress of shopping, rushing, and cooking or feel that the whole thing is just way too commercial these days, can't help but smile with some holiday spirit.

It's easy to get caught up in the fast pace of modern life, do all your shopping online, and limit your decorating to setting the table before dinner. For many of us, time is a precious and rare commodity. But to take a little time to focus on the joys of this season can create a rich and beautiful experience, allowing us to recapture a little of the magick of the season that we knew as children.

This is a magickal time of year, evidenced by the similar myths that abound from all over the globe. On this shortest day of the year, the Sun symbolically dies and is reborn. The Child of Light returns to the world, bringing longer days from this point on. Fire and light festivals are common throughout the world as are holiday plays, parties, movies, and other events.

This time of year brings with it an excitement that is rarely surpassed by another holiday season, particularly for children. Why not get involved with the joy of the season by crafting your own decorations and gifts or simply making a yummy treat to share with friends?

Altars and Sacred Space

The creation of altars and sacred space in this chapter revolve around the Sun. As a solar event and a time of year when most of us are feeling some cold, the Winter Solstice is an ideal time to bring in light and warmth through magickal crafts, as we spiral through time into the new year.

Embossed Altar Cloth

Embossed velvet has the look of pure luxury, yet these impressed patterns are surprisingly easy to create. Embossed Celtic knotwork cloths can be seen in several places on our cover. Velvet brings through a rich, glowing warmth that is ideal for this time of year. The embossed sections catch the light of fires and candles, adding a unique sparkle to the lights and decorations of Yule.

Materials

- velvet rayon
- cotton fabric for backing
- cotton dishcloth
- iron
- double-sided bias tape
- spray starch
- needle
- thread
- rubber stamps (see the Crafts section in this chapter to make your own)

1. To make a 24 foot by 24 foot altar cloth, cut out a 24-foot square of velvet. Adjust the size and shape to fit your altar.

2. Place a rubber stamp face-up on a firm flat surface. Carefully lay the velvet, plush side down, over the rubber stamp, where you want the pattern to be impressed. Leave a 3-inch border around the edge to allow for finishing.

3. Lightly spray an even layer of starch onto the back of the velvet. Gently place the clean, dry, cotton dishcloth on top of the velvet to protect both velvet and iron.

4. Using a hot iron, press down firmly over the cloth, velvet, and stamp for 12 seconds. Be careful not to move the rubber stamp and velvet until the embossed pattern is complete. Repeat as necessary.

5. Repeat Steps 1 through 4 with various stamps until you are happy with the overall design.

6. Cut out a 24-foot square cotton cloth to use as a backing for your altar cloth. With wrong sides together, baste stitch all around the edge.

8. Sew a ¼-inch hem along the outer edge.

9. Pin double-sided bias tape around the edge of the square. Sew in place with a zigzag or blanket stitch.

NOTE: We recommend that you practice your embossing technique on a scrap of velvet before working on your altar cloth.

Spiral of the Sun

Imagine a glowing spiral laid out before you. Friends and family carry their own candles on a walking meditation through the spiral. This is a beautiful and sacred experience that everyone can feel. We did something similar for a group of homeschoolers in 2004 and even the 3-year-olds were quiet and calm by the time they reached the center.

This is a variation on the traditional labyrinth idea. The spiral represents many things to many people. It is continuity, inner mysteries, spiritual transformation, and the movement of energy throughout the body. For our purposes here, the journey in and out of the spiral represents the death and rebirth of the Sun. The lighting of many candles from the one candle is symbolic of the rebirth of the Sun and the lengthening of days. As each person lights another candle your spiral of light shines brighter.

Building the Spiral

1. Lay out a large spiral in your yard or park. Unless you want to use an AutoCAD system or mathematically calculate the spiral design, we recommend just walking a spiral and marking your path with small stones. You can adjust the path before proceeding if you want.

2. Widen your path to create a 2-foot-wide walkway using evergreen branches or yellow cord strung with gold stars as the walkway walls. If you are fortunate enough to have snow for Yule, then you can make a beautiful spiral labyrinth by simply digging a walkway in the snow.

3. Place lighted candle lanterns (see the next section) or luminarias (see the Kids Stuff section in this chapter) every 2 to 3 feet along the edges of the walkway.

4. Place a small altar in the center with a single lighted, gold candle.

Candle Lantern

These clever lanterns bring a warm glow to any Yule celebration. Not only are they great fun for all ages to make, but they also offer you the chance to recycle your old jars and turn them into keepsakes for years to come. Take this opportunity to really personalize the light and shadow in your home at this time of year.

Materials	
• glass jar with wide mouth	• glue gun
• wire cutters	• heavy-gauge wire
• tea light	• decorations: stickers, paint, etc.
	• optional: pliers

1. Decorate your glass jar with paint, stickers, and whatever else you fancy.

2. Cut a long length of wire, approximately 4 feet long for a 16-ounce jar. Twist a small loop in the center of the wire.

3. Hold the loop to the rim of the jar and bend the two long arms of wire around the neck of the jar.

4. Twist the two arms of wire tightly together directly opposite the wire loop. Then twist the remaining wire together, forming the lantern's handle.

5. Bend the handle into shape and fasten securely through the opposite loop. Take care to tuck the wire ends snugly against the handle.

6. Glue the tea light in the center of the inside bottom of the lantern.

Walking the Spiral

Before beginning, have each person pick up an unlit candle on a candleholder or a candle with a wax-guard. Waiting a few seconds between people, walk to the center of the spiral. You may want to empty your mind as you walk or focus on the year that is ending and what you hope for the new year. An adult should accompany young children.

Light your candle from the central altar candle and give thanks for the rebirth of the Sun. This is also a good time to state any resolutions you might have for the new year.

When you have completed the spiral walk, either extinguish your candle to relight at home or place your lit candle on a community solstice altar.

Tools and Oracles

Have you ever listened to snow gently falling in a quiet forest? It barely makes a sound and yet it creates a feeling of being outside of space and time: a truly magickal winter wonderland. At Winter Solstice, we bring you tools reminiscent of snowy nights and evergreen trees. Though you may use an altar chalice and your favorite divination system all year round, it might be fun to experiment with something different this year and align your magick even more with the season of snow and light.

Frosted Glass Chalice

This is a beautiful chalice you can design yourself—with frosted glass, of course. You can see a frosted triple moon chalice in the composite photo in the center of our cover. Imagine yourself as the Winter Queen or King holding a goblet of snow and ice. Or perhaps you are a winter witch, scrying in a magick snowball. Whatever fun ideas spark your imagination, you can create them through the designs on your chalice.

Materials

- wine glass
- sticky-back plastic or stickers
- pencil
- etching cream
- paper
- scissors
- old paintbrush

1. After planning your chalice design on a piece of paper, sketch or trace your design onto the sticky-back plastic.
2. Clean the chalice with warm soapy water and dry completely.
3. Cut out the sticky-back plastic shapes and stick them firmly onto the chalice. If you are using stickers, secure them to the chalice now and press out any bubbles.
4. Following the etching cream manufacturer's instructions carefully, paint a layer of etching cream all over the bowl of your glass chalice, covering the plastic, and leave on as directed.
5. Gently rinse off the etching cream with warm water.
6. Repeat steps 4 and 5 if necessary.
7. Peel off stickers.

NOTE: Etching cream is a highly toxic substance and should be handled with caution. Use it in a well-ventilated area, cover your work area with newspaper, and wear gloves and eye protection.

Runes

The runes are an ancient Norse magickal alphabet. In the same way that the Celtic ogham and other magickal scripts do, the runes embody universal forces and specific energies. It is said that Odinn hung from a tree to receive this wisdom. Some say the tree was an ash; others say it was a type of evergreen. In any event, they are associated with magickal trees, much like the Winter Solstice.

	Quick Guide to the Runes	
ᚠ	Fehu	money, property, power, fertility
ᚢ	Uruz	manifestation, strength, vitality, health
ᚦ	Thurisaz	destruction, defense, regeneration
ᚨ	Ansuz	reception, transformation, inspiration
ᚱ	Raidho	travel, ritual, cosmic order
ᚲ	Kenaz	transformation, sexuality, creativity
ᚷ	Gebo	gifts, ecstasy, relationships
ᚹ	Wunjo	joy, harmony, fellowship
ᚺ	Hagalaz	protection, completion, testing
ᚾ	Naudhiz	necessity, resistance, deliverance
ᛁ	Isa	ego, challenge, concentration
ᛃ	Jera	year, reward, fruition
ᛇ	Eihwaz	life and death, rebirth, reliability, protection
ᛈ	Perthro	divination, change, cause and effect
ᛉ	Algiz	protection, defense, spiritual sanctuary
ᛊ	Sowilo	life force, health, success, magickal will
ᛏ	Tiwaz	justice, self-sacrifice, spiritual discipline
ᛒ	Berkano	Earth Mother, birth, rites of passage
ᛖ	Ehwaz	loyalty, marriage, shamanic journeying
ᛗ	Mannaz	intelligence, divine structure, the Self
ᛚ	Laguz	water, guidance, dreams
ᛜ	Ingwaz	potential, relief, gestation
ᛞ	Dagaz	light, polarity, breakthrough
ᛟ	Othala	prosperity, security, inheritance

The crafting of your own magickal tools is an amazing experience that truly attunes you to your working tools. This can become an excellent teaching opportunity as well. Study the runes as you plan your creation. Meditate on the meaning of each rune as you form its shape to deepen your connection to and your understanding of the runes.

Materials

- 4 blocks of polymer clay: 3 blocks of the same color and 1 in a contrasting color
- glass baking dish

1. Divide the 3 same-colored blocks of polymer clay for the runes in 8 equal-sized pieces, making a total of 24 pieces.
2. Form the body of the rune by rolling the clay into a ball between your palms. Press your palms gently down on the clay rune ball, until you are happy with its shape.
3. Make the rune letters with the contrasting clay by rolling out small, thin sausages of clay and placing them gently on the rune body in the shape of the rune letter.
4. When you are happy with the shape of the rune letter, press it firmly but gently into the clay body.
5. Follow the clay manufacturer's directions for baking.

Crafts

Have you ever received a handmade gift? Do you remember how touched you were that someone put the time, thought, and energy into making something just for you? Wouldn't it be wonderful to give that same feeling to your loved ones? This is the idea behind all the Winter Solstice crafts. They can be simple enough to do with kids or intricate enough to do yourself and sell at a festival.

Holiday Wreaths

This is the season for holiday wreaths and they may be found in nearly every nursery, craft store, grocery store, and Christmas tree lot at this time of year. But did you know they are fairly simple and great fun to make? What a wonderful way to add a personal touch (and a little magick) to a pretty standard holiday decoration. Be sure to give thanks to the trees and plants you are using to craft your wreath.

```
┌─ Materials ─┐
```

- floral wire
- glue gun
- 12–14-inch base: Styrofoam circle or wire ring
- filler: fir or pine branches, holly and ivy, etc.
- decorations: pine cones, plastic ornaments, glitter, ribbons, spirit animal pendants, etc.

NOTE: For a little extra energy, try using one of the magickal herbs listed later in this chapter or a special symbol in your wreath.

1. Wire the filler to the base. Be sure to use enough filler to cover the entire form of the base. This can be a beautiful wreath without adding any decorations.

2. Wire or glue the decorations to the filler and the base. If you are using a Styrofoam base, many decorations may be simply poked into or glued to the Styrofoam. Decorative ribbon may be used to tie decorations to the greenery.

Stamp Carving

Although many copyright-free designs are available online or already cut into stamps at craft stores, how much more personal and powerful must it be to create your own designs for altar cloths, cloaks, or anything you might want to stamp and emboss? These stamps are also ideal for use with ink to create unique decorative holiday cards. Simply print, photocopy, or sketch out some designs that resonate with you (perhaps the outline of your totem animal or favorite deity).

```
┌─ Materials ─┐
```

- stamp block
- printed copy of the image
- cotton ball
- acetone nail polish remover
- tracing paper
- pencil
- craft knife

Selecting the Block

Vinyl erasers make a good small-scale stamp. This size is perfect for making embossed velvet bags.

A rubber gasket made for sinks usually measures 6 inches by 6 inches and makes a great medium-sized stamp. This relatively dense rubber allows for a surprising amount of detailed carving. Kristin uses this for some of her more complex drum head designs.

Liz's favorite larger-scale stamping medium is 12" × 18" Soft-Kut printing blocks (available online from *www.dickblick.com*). With these, you can make a velvet cloak into an original piece of art.

Transferring the Image

1. Lay a printed copy of the image face-down on the stamp.
2. Firmly press a cotton ball dampened with acetone nail polish remover onto the back of the paper until the image has been successfully transferred.

NOTE: Because this method of transfer will give you a mirror image, you may need to use tracing paper. Trace your image on one side of the paper. On the opposite side, retrace the image. Placing this second side down on the stamp, go over the image one final time. The graphite from the other side will leave a thin line on your stamp with the correct image facing you.

Carving the Block

Holding your blade as you would a pencil, firmly cut around your design. Keep the blade at a 25-degree angle, making slow shallow cuts and cutting away more as necessary.

Test your stamp out on a scrap of velvet before using on your final project.

NOTE: Always carve away from your body and keep your blades sharp.

Herbal Gift Soaps

Handmade herbal soaps are a real treat! These transform the everyday job of taking a bath or shower into a spa-like pleasure of soothing scents and skin-nourishing herbs and oils. What a fabulous gift to give a loved one at Yule!

You need not mess with lye and complex soap-making techniques to craft magickal soaps for family and friends. Simply buy bricks of glycerin or olive oil soap at your local hobby store or recycle old scraps from unscented bars of soap around your home and rework them to make beautiful gifts. This craft can be as elaborate or as simple as you choose, and children love to help out.

┌─────────────────────┐
│   Materials   │
└─────────────────────┘

- 10-ounce glycerin or olive oil soap
- herbs for fragrance or magick
- mold (You can make your own molds from plastic containers or other open shapes. Use plastic wrap to prevent sticking.)

1. Heat the soap according to the manufacturer's directions. If you are using leftover soap bars, grate them in a blender and add a small amount of water. Then heat until it reaches a watery paste-like consistency. This takes approximately 40 seconds in a microwave.

2. Add color or herbs and mix well.

3. Pour into mold and allow to cool at least 30 minutes.

4. Using even pressure on all sides, force the soap from the mold and wrap it in holiday gift wrap or a box. Be sure to include a card noting the meanings of the colors and herbs used.

Magickal Herbs	
Angelica	protection, purification, visioning
Bay	protection, purification, love, strength, visioning
Chamomile	relaxing, calming, soothing
Cinnamon	spirituality, healing, prosperity, visioning
Eucalyptus	healing, protection
Honeysuckle	protection, prosperity, visioning
Lavendar	protection, purification, dreaming, love, peace
Rose	love, protection, purification, dreaming, peace
Rosemary	love, protection, purification, visioning, healing
Sage	protection, visioning, wisdom
Violet	protection, love, peace, visioning

Gift papers

Making paper has been a family favorite around the Madden house for years. We've crafted magickal papers, stationary, memory books (see Chapter 12), journal covers, and picture frames—all from a variety of homemade paper. This is a wonderful way to create something special for loved ones as you learn about the process and about recycling. We use everything from used copy and wrapping paper to egg cartons and old clothes.

As with all handmade gifts, homemade paper brings with it the energy of the love you put into it. Just as soap can, it can be personalized with specific colors and herbs for each person. But more than that, gift papers can be designed with magick in mind. Imagine the look on your friends' faces as they open a box of paper for prosperity spells, protection, or even love spells! This is the extra bit of magick you can add to this craft that will benefit your loved ones year-round.

Materials

- blender or food processor
- sponge
- bits of non-glossy paper, old egg cartons, or cardboard torn into small pieces
- screen with frame: window screening stapled to a picture frame will do
- tub or bucket large enough to submerge the frame
- stack of newspapers covered with a towel or other cloth
- optional: iron for smoothing, liquid starch to prevent ink from soaking in too much
- cookie cutter for special designs, magickal herbs
- for color and texture: bleach, food coloring, pieces of leaves or flowers, glitter, etc.

1. Soak the bits of paper in hot water for about 30 minutes.

2. Blend the soaked paper into a pulp until there are no pieces of paper left. Add optional bleach or coloring and blend in.

3. Fill the tub with water and add the pulp in a ratio of 4 parts water to 1 part pulp.

   More pulp will make a thicker paper, and you can experiment with this ratio. Mix this so the pulp is floating in the water. If you want to use liquid starch, add 1 to 2 teaspoons now and mix well. Add any textures, glitter, or flowers and swirl to swirl them about.

4. Submerge the screen in the tub. Slowly raise the screen to the top of the water. Hold it just over the surface and allow most of the water to drain. If you want a thicker or thinner paper, this is the time to add or remove pulp.

5. Carefully turn the screen over onto the stack of newspapers. Use the sponge to absorb as much water as you can.

6. Gently lift the screen, removing the paper very carefully. If the paper sticks, it is either too wet or you pulled too quickly. Press out bubbles or tears.

7. If you are using a cookie cutter, cut the paper into the desired shapes now and peel off any extra paper.

8. Cover with another cloth and more newspaper for 24 hours.

9. Remove the newspaper and allow it to dry for another 24 hours in a clean, dry place.

10. Iron on low heat once it is fully dry.

Magickal Delicacies

The foods and drinks at this time of year are responsible for much of the dieting that takes place in January. There is just so much to taste and savor! Be healthy, but remember that some treats are truly good for the soul. Here we offer you two traditional favorites, one from Scandinavia and one from Britain. We hope you enjoy them as much as we do.

Jul (Yule) Glögg

This is THE Scandinavian beverage for the Yule season. Many a family has warmed up with the glögg and danced the night away. Aquavit may be difficult to find in some areas, so you might consider substituting vodka or schnapps, though it really isn't the same!

Materials

- 1 liter aquavit (or substitute)
- 1 bottle dry red wine
- 1 tablespoon ground cardamom
- 5 cloves
- 2 orange peels
- 1 cup blanched almonds
- 1 cup raisins
- 3 cinnamon sticks
- optional: 3–5 sugar cubes
- matches
- large pot with cover

1. Combine all ingredients except sugar cubes in large pot. Heat to boiling, then reduce heat to simmer. Add sugar cubes and simmer for at least 30 minutes.

2. Remove from heat and light with a match. Allow to burn for 30 seconds and cover to extinguish flame.

Figgie Pudding

A famous song begs someone to give us some Figgie Pudding. Traditionally, Figgie Pudding is placed on the center of the festive table, where it is then saturated in brandy and immediately set alight with a match. A second tradition that belongs with this richly flavored dish is to add a lucky sixpence. The one who finds the lucky sixpence will be blessed with good fortune. Unlike the fruitcake that has become the butt of many a joke, the flavor of Figgie Pudding improves with age and so it is often made several months ahead of time.

Materials

• 1 cup raisins	• 1 teaspoon ground mixed spice
• 1 cup sultanas	• ½ teaspoon grated nutmeg
• ½ cup cranberries	• mixing bowl
• ¼ cup chopped pitted prunes	• glass or ceramic bowl
• ¼ cup chopped apricots	• oil
• 4 ounces stout ale	• electric mixer
• juice and rind of 1 lemon	• greaseproof paper
• ¾ cup butter	• string
• 1 cup of brown sugar	• large pan
• 3 eggs	• ½–1 cup heavy cream
• 1 cup bread crumbs	• aluminum foil
• ¼ cup chopped almonds	• shot of brandy

1. Mix fruit, ale, lemon juice and rind together. Cover and leave overnight.

2. Cream butter and sugar together until fluffy.

3. Beat eggs.

4. Mix all the ingredients up to nutmeg together and press into an oiled glass or ceramic bowl (allow room for expansion).

5. Cut a circle of greaseproof paper 4 inches wider than the top of your bowl. Oil the paper and place over the top of your pudding bowl.

6. Hold the greaseproof paper in place with a circle of tin foil scrunched to form a lid. Secure with string around the neck of the bowl.

7. Place bowl in a large pan of water. Steam for 6 hours adding water as needed.

8. Before serving, reheat by steaming for a further 1½ hours.

9. Serve with heavy cream, whipped up with a little brandy.

Traditions From Around the World

Lucia Day honors the Christian martyr Saint Lucia, who is said to have brought food to persecuted Christians hiding in caves in fourth-century Sicily. She lit her way through the caves with torches tied around her head. Some believe that she visited Sweden and gained the love of the Swedish people. Others find a connection with the goddess Freya in the Lucia's Cats (yummy treats) that are so special at this time of year and believe that She, as did the Celtic Brighid, took on a Christian form so that She might survive into modern times.

Before the Gregorian calendar, Winter Solstice fell on December 13th. In Sweden, Lucia Day begins the Christmas season on December 13th. Before dawn, the eldest daughter, wearing a white robe and her crown of candles, carries a breakfast of coffee, gingerbread, and sweet rolls (Lucia's Cats or Buns) to each person in the household. The Lucia crown is a circular ring decorated with greenery and four candles or holiday lights. The daughter may be accompanied by the Star Boys, wearing white robes with white cone-shaped hats with golden stars and carrying star wands.

Candle Wreath

Although this is a wonderful tradition, few people today want to go through the trouble of getting the family up early enough for it, and, to be honest, wearing the Lucia crown can take some practice. So we adapted the idea for use as an altar piece or table decoration. This brings a beautifully warm and sparkling feel to any celebration.

Materials	
• 6–8-inch Styrofoam circle or wire ring	• floral wire
	• decorations: pine cones or shiny gold stars
• evergreen branches	
• 4 white taper candles	• optional: glue gun

1. Place holders for the candles at each of the four directions to form an equal-armed cross. For a Styrofoam ring, cut candle-sized holes into the foam. For a wire ring, use the floral wire to create a candle-sized spiral that will hold the candles erect. Place your candles in to test this before adding the greens and decorations. It must hold the candles firmly.

2. With candles in place, wire the branches to the wire ring or Styrofoam circle so that they completely cover the entire form of the base.

3. Wire or glue the decorations on and allow glue to dry completely before lighting the candles.

Kid Stuff

The Yule season is made even more fun for kids by playing games, singing songs, and making decorations and other crafts. Young children enjoy making or helping to make special handcrafted gifts for family and friends. But the act of decorating is possibly the most fun of all, at least for children. The home and yard are transformed into a wonderland of colors and lights that only adds to the excitement of the season. Luminarias are a fairly simple craft for kids, though they do require some adult assistance. Even Liz's 1-year-old had fun splashing around the paint on them.

Luminarias

These little lights adorn many American Southwest homes at Yule, cheering up the winter nights and reminding us of the coming light. In Santa Fe and Albuquerque, holiday luminaria tours attract thousands of people from all over the country. Sometimes made of punched tin or plastic, traditional luminarias (also known as farolitos) are made with paper bags, sand, and candles.

| Materials |

- play sand
- votive candles
- paper lunch bags (Brown is traditional, but you might experiment with other colors.)

- optional: stencils, pencil, and scissors or craft knife (use with adult supervision only)
- watercolor paint and paintbrush

1. Trace or stencil your design on the bag. You might like a star or sun design, or perhaps you prefer a peace sign, pentacle, or yin/yang. Have an adult or older child cut the design out with scissors or a craft knife.

2. Paint each bag with your chosen design.

3. Fill each paper bag with 2–3 inches of sand.

4. Put the bag in place in your yard or room. Place a votive candle snugly in the sand.

5. Roll the top of the bag down 2 or 3 inches. Light the candle with long matches or a long lighter. Never leave a lit candle unattended.

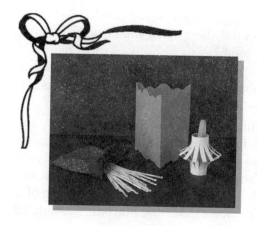

Chapter 4

Imbolc

I mbolc offers us the magick of birth and new beginnings. You can almost feel the buds and flowers stretching, pushing up toward the light. Think of a beautiful gift, the moment before it is unwrapped—you can sense the exhilaration before the great blossoming of spring.

This is a perfect time for planting seeds, not only in the earth but also in your life. Now is a good time to make plans and go forward with your dreams. Take a few moments to consider what harvests you reaped last year. Try to see how you planted and fed those seeds. Start a list of what dreams you hope to grow this year and make concrete plans for how to plant and nurture these new seeds.

Because Imbolc is Brighid's feast day, many of the crafts and food in this chapter are dedicated to Her. She is sometimes seen as a triple goddess. Even those who do not perceive Her in this way certainly recognize Her threefold aspects as the patroness of poetry, smith-craft, and healing.

Altars and Sacred Space

This is the first of the spring festivals and a wonderful time to re-evaluate your altar or how you honor the spirit beings that bless and protect you. Does your altar need cleaning? Perhaps it is time to spruce it up or add something new. Maybe you'd like a new altar or a portable one. These are the ideas behind our sacred space offerings for Imbolc.

Retablo to Brighid

Retablos are a type of *santos,* meaning "holy person" or "holy object." Retablo translates as "painted panel." These saintly images developed from a rich Spanish tradition of crafting highly decorative images for worship. These retablos decorated the homes and churches of the Spanish colonists. Traditionally, a retablo was painted on small pieces of wood or tin. The wood pieces were cut from pine and then a smooth coating was applied before the image was painted with various colors, often made from ground pigments of native plants and clay.

Modern retablos make beautiful altar pieces to depict and honor any deity or spirit ally. This version is made from a pine board and painted with acrylic paints. You may choose to make a single-panel piece or a three-panel hinged version that will fold closed or stand alone as described. The three-panel version is equally suitable for the depiction of a triple aspect deity or three personal deities. See the bottom right side of our cover for both versions of a Brighid retablo.

Materials

- pencil and paper
- sandpaper
- gesso acrylic primer
- acrylic paints
- small paintbrush
- acrylic coating
- 4 brass hinges: 1" × 1"
- screwdriver
- 2 rectangles of pine: 5" × 7" × 1"
- 1 rectangle of pine: 10" × 7" × 1"

1. Design your own image or choose one from a book to represent your favorite deity or spirit guide. Sketch or trace your designs on paper to the same scale as the panels.
2. Use the sandpaper to make rounded edges on each panel.
3. Paint a smooth, even layer of gesso on the front of each panel.
4. After the gesso has dried, lightly sketch or trace the outline of your design on each panel.
5. Paint the image with acrylic paints.
6. Protect the image with a layer of acrylic coating.
7. Place the spine of the hinges on the painted side of the panels, 1 inch from the top and bottom edges, and screw it in place with the large panel in the center.

Hand-Painted Box Altar

Many people have a personal altar-in-a-box. Whether cardboard, plastic, or wood, these allow their owners to store candles and other magickal items for travel or privacy. In many cases, they also serve as the base for a small (and portable) altar. This pine box may also serve as a memory box or a type of medicine pouch, holding the special gifts you have received from Spirit.

Materials

- sandpaper or sponge
- pencil and paper
- tracing paper
- pine wood box

- gesso or primer paint
- acrylic paints
- paintbrushes
- acrylic varnish

1. Clean off any sticky residue from labels with a damp sponge or sandpaper.
2. Sketch out your design to scale. Astrological symbols, power animals, special plants or other symbols are wonderful ways to personalize your box.
3. Paint on the base coat of gesso or primer paint and allow it to dry completely.
4. Trace your design onto the tracing paper. Then transfer the image onto your altar.
5. Paint your design on to your altar and allow to dry completely.
6. Finish with a coat of acrylic varnish.

Tools and Oracles

Cleansing and purification are on the list for this festival. As we begin to emerge from the long darkness, sometimes we need to clear out the dust in order to see the light returning. Once we do that, it is time to peer into the coming year and do some traditional Celtic divination.

Smudge Fan

You can use smudge to clear the cobwebs from your home and mind after the long winter. Cultures throughout the world have used burning herbs for purification and sending prayers to the gods. Fans for smudge can be as simple as folded paper or a single feather. They can also be incredibly elaborate, combining many feathers of different sizes and shapes with inlaid wood or bone and beading. Here, we offer you something in between.

Materials

- 1–3 feathers
- 1 piece of wood or bone
- drill and bit or sharp, sturdy knife
- glue

- optional: small bit of clay or modeling compound
- optional decorations: small cabochons of stone, beads, ribbons, markers, etc.

1. First ensure that your wood or bone is large enough to accommodate the number of feathers you wish to use. Feather shafts tend to be ¼ inch or less in width. It is best to leave ⅛ to ¼ inch around the outside edge of the handle so it does not crack or break. If you are adding inlaid stones to the handle, add at least another ⅛ inch to the width of the edge.

   For example, a fan containing one feather that has a ¼ inch wide shaft and no inlaid stones should have a ¼-inch hole drilled into a handle at least ¾ inch wide.

2. Arrange the feathers as you want them to look and measure the total width of the shafts. Then measure how deep you want the feathers to go into the handle. This will tell you the width and depth of the hole you need to drill or cut into the handle.

3. Drill or cut the hole into the handle. If you want to use clay to hold the feathers in place until the glue dries, add an extra ¼ inch of depth to your hole.

4. If you plan to add small stones to the handle, carve out a hollow the size of the stone. Keep this as shallow as possible unless you have a thick edge around the hole of your handle.

5. Insert the feathers into the handle to be sure it is the correct width and depth. Adjust the hole as necessary. Remove the feathers.

6. Fill the bottom of the hole with glue and reinsert the feathers. Add additional glue into the hole as needed. Hold the feathers in place until the glue is fairly dry. Allow to dry completely in a safe place where the feathers will not be pushed or pulled out of place.

7. Glue the stones into any hollows you carved. You may also wish to decorate the fan by adding a ribbon or wire, beadwork, or magickal symbols.

Smudge Ceremony

Often considered a Native American ceremony, similar methods have been used throughout the world for purification and opening to the spirit world. Whether you go traditional and use sagebrush with sweetgrass or create your own tradition with rosemary, lavender, or lemongrass, this ceremony will touch your heart and soul and set the stage for truly sacred space.

Materials

- matches or a lighter
- heat-resistant container (see Chapter 10)
- smudge fan
- magickal herbs (see Chapter 3)

1. Take a moment to center yourself. It may help to count yourself down from 10 to 1, remembering to breathe deeply.

2. Light the herbs with respect and ask that the smoke purify your energy and this space.

3. Using your fan to move the smoke, offer the sacred smoke to the directions, to the Earth and Sky, and to the Creator or Great Spirit in the center. Offer blessings of respect and gratitude to each of these.

4. Beginning at your heart or navel, bathe yourself in the sacred and purifying smoke. Move the smoke up over your head, along your back, down to your feet, and back up to your heart or navel. Some people like to "wash" their faces, hands, and feet in the smoke.

5. As the smoke moves along your body, feel yourself relax and center. Breathe deeply of the smoke, if it does not irritate your throat and lungs. See your worries and tensions dissolve in the warmth as they are carried up and away by the smoke. Carry your smudge around your home. Be sure to encourage the smoke into every corner, every grate and crevice, under every bed, and around all doors and windows.

6. Offer the smoke once more to each of the directions, to Earth and Sky, and to the Creator. Thank them for their presence in your life. Thank the smoke of these sacred herbs for their assistance in purifying your energy.

Ogham

The ogham script is an ancient Celtic tree alphabet that was used as a method of communication and as a magickal mnemonic device, similar to the runes of the Germanic/Norse and the Qabbalah of the Hebrew mystics. Ogma, son of King Elatha of Ireland, is credited with its invention. Apparently Ogma was a skilled Bard and the ogham was believed to be a language of the other worlds. One story relates that Ogma was inspired by the flight of cranes and saw the beginnings of the ogham script in the way they held their legs in flight.

Ogham Sticks

As can the runes, the ogham may be used as a divination system. We have both used ogham sticks that we created ourselves. At face value, they appear simple but they are surprisingly accurate and powerful—plus they are fun and different.

The first step is to obtain the wood for your ogham sticks. You may want to collect each of the sacred woods that are associated with the ogham "letters." Or you may prefer to buy large lollipop or craft sticks.

We suggest seeking a branch or twigs to make your sticks from in Nature, maybe at a park or forest or even in your own back yard. Venture out on a walk with the sole intent to find the wood that is right for you and your ogham. Go where you are led and try to choose straight, dry twigs about 6 inches long or a suitable fallen branch that can be cut to an appropriate size. Remember to give thanks to the tree that dropped your sticks! Offerings of water or simple blessings are always appreciated by the Nature spirits.

Materials

- twenty 6-inch sticks of wood
- fine sandpaper
- pencil
- wood-burning tool
- wood oil
- cotton rag

---

1. Sand the rough edges on each stick with sandpaper. Pencil 1 ogham name and its symbol along with the corresponding tree name and letter of your usual alphabet along one side of each stick. Turn the stick over and pencil in 1 or 2 words that represent the associations of that ogham.

2. Heat up your wood-burning tool in a safe place away from little hands and paws. Follow your pencil lines to burn the words and characters permanently onto each disk.

3. Finish off each disk with light coat of wood oil, rubbed in with a cotton cloth.

	The Ogham Script		
	Irish	**English**	**Divinatory associations**
⊢	*Beith*	Birch	new beginnings, purification
⊨	*Luis*	Rowan	divination, protection
⊨	*Fearn*	Alder	foundation, ancestors
⊨	*Saille*	Willow	intuition, life lessons
⊨	*Nuin*	Ash	interconnections, linking inner and outer worlds
⊣	*Huathe*	Hawthorn	cleansing, protection
⊣	*Duir*	Oak	doorway, endurance
⊣	*Tinne*	Holly	justice, directed effort
⊣	*Coll*	Hazel	wisdom, creativity
⊣	*Quert*	Apple	the Otherworld, eternity
✛	*Muinn*	Vine	the line between knowledge and madness, visioning
✛	*Gort*	Ivy	transformation, beauty
✛	*Ngetal*	Reed	harmony, generosity
✛	*Straif*	Blackthorn	fate, unexpected change
✛	*Ruis*	Elder	transition, end of a cycle
✛	*Ailm*	Fir/Pine	strength, opportunity
✛	*Onn*	Gorse	gathering, wisdom
✛	*Ur*	Heather	unity, healing
✛	*Edhadh*	Aspen	truth, overcoming adversity
✛	*Ido*	Yew	rebirth, immortality

Crafts

Divination, flame, and herb—these are the crafts of Imbolc. Whether you craft them for yourself or give them as a gift to a loved one, you bring through the energies of the Goddess and this festival as you create and play with these ideas.

Ogham Bag

Kristin keeps her ogham sticks in a beautiful embossed green velvet bag with a green-gold inner lining that Liz made for her. Pulling the sticks from this very special bag gives her the feeling of being an ancient druid, divining matters of great importance for an honored king or queen.

This easy pattern makes a great ogham bag. Choose some nice material for the lining as well as the outer bag because the top edge of the lining becomes a decorative cuff. Add beads and ribbons or a tassel trim to jazz it up or change the dimensions of this pattern to make the perfect bag for any of your magickal treasures. This is a very special bag. Allow the awen (*pron.* AH-oo-en), or divine inspiration, to flow through you as you create it.

Materials

- pins
- cotton thread
- needle
- safety pin

- 2 lengths of thin twist cord or ribbon, each 20" long
- 2 rectangles of cotton material: 12" × 9" for the outer bag
- 2 rectangles of cotton material: 12" × 9" for the lining
- optional: sewing machine

1. With right sides together, pin the 2 pieces of outer fabric together along the bottom edge and long sides.

2. Stitch along sides and lower edges. Turn bag right side out.

3. Pin right sides of the lining together.

4. Stitch along the sides leaving a 1-inch opening between 3½ and 4½ inches from the top edge.

5. Slip the outer bag inside the lining so that the right sides of each are facing each other. Stitch the bag and lining together at the upper edge.

6. Turn the bag right-side out. Slipstitch the lower edges of the lining together.

7. Sew a circle of stitching around the bag at top and bottom of side holes forming a tube for the cord.

8. Use the safety pin to thread 1 cord or ribbon through the tube, all the way though the bag and back out of the same side. Tie the ends together. Repeat on the opposite side with the second cord.

Floating Candles

At one time, people would divine the future by dropping hot lead or wax into water and reading the resultant shapes. Today, many people use candles to set a special mood or gaze into their flames as a form of meditation. Because Brighid is a goddess of both fire and water, floating candles are a beautiful and appropriate decoration for this time of year. If you want to use some extra wax to drip into the water, try this chant and see what images you can find as the wax cools:

> Brighid, Goddess of the Light
> Bring me now the Second Sight.
> Bless my mind and help me see
> Make my visions clear to me.

Materials

- small pot of water
- tin can
- box of clean, damp sand (large enough to leave a wall of sand at least 1 inch thick around your candle)
- lead-free wicks
- paraffin wax or leftover candle stubs with the wicks removed

1. Carve out a wide and shallow shape for your candle in the damp sand.

2. Place the wax in the tin can. If you are using more than one color, place each color in its own can.

3. Add about 1 inch of water to the pot and place the can containing the wax in it. Melt the wax in the water over medium to high heat. Do not allow it to boil.

4. Place the wick into the center of the sand mold and pour the wax into the carved-out space around the wick. Be very careful as melted wax can burn your skin. If you want different colors in your candle, allow the first color to cool and solidify before adding the next color.

5. Allow to cool completely before removing from the sand.

6. Float in a bowl of water and light your candles.

Garden Circle

The creation of a garden circle is a powerful way to work with the energies of Imbolc. To plant a sacred grove or a ritual circle of herbs and flowers is to create a sacred temple on your own land. If you do have the time and space, we encourage you to plant native plants whenever possible. Use the chart on page 63 to gain some ideas for the plants whose energies might resonate best with your circle and your home. (The elements and some of the planets and other associations were taken from Scott Cunninghamn's *Encyclopedia of Magical Herbs* [Llewellyn, 1993].)

Paint a Potted Herb Garden

Even those of us with little or no land can enjoy a magickal garden circle. Container gardens are becoming more and more popular these days, making it possible for even apartment-dwellers to bring the energies of the natural world into their homes. With potted plants, you can easily create a sacred circle of plants, or of plants and stones, whenever you meditate or hold a ritual.

Materials

- terra-cotta pots
- washing liquid
- pencil
- acrylic paints
- paintbrushs
- oil
- optional: rubber stamps (see Chapter 3) or stencils
- seeds and soil

1. Wash, rinse, and dry the terra-cotta pots thoroughly.
2. Sketch, stencil, or stamp your design on each pot.
3. Paint your design and let it dry.
4. Add soil and seed(s).
5. Give it the right amount of sunshine, water, and tender loving care.

Magickal Delicacies

Any kitchen witch will tell you that there is nothing more magickal than creating yummy delights to share with friends and family. The sights, smells, textures, and tastes of magickal delicacies involve one's entire being in a spell of joy and pleasure. These Imbolc treats are dedicated to the goddess Brighid and her Celtic worshippers.

Magickal Plant	Element/ Plant	Other Associations
Angelica	fire/Sun	protection, healing, visioning, purification
Basil	fire/Mars	protection, wealth, love, purification
Blackberry	water/Neptune	protection, healing, wealth
Cactus	fire/Sun	protection, purification
Catnip	water/Venus	love, beauty, happiness, protection
Clover	air/Uranus	protection, wealth, love, success
Comfrey	water/Saturn	protection, wealth, safety during travel
Daisy	water/Venus	love, happiness
Dandelion	air/Jupiter	divination, healing, spirit communication
Fern	earth/Mercury	protection, healing, wealth, purification
Holly	fire/Mars	protection, luck, dreaming
Honeysuckle	earth/Jupiter	protection, wealth, psychic powers
Lavender	air/Mercury	protection, love, happiness, purification, peace
Lemon Balm	water/Moon	love, success, healing
Lily of the Valley	air/Mercury	happiness, mental powers
Mint	air/Pluto	healing, wealth, purification
Mugwort	earth/Moon	protection, healing, visioning, dreaming
Primrose	earth/Venus	protection, love
Rosemary	fire/Sun	protection, healing, love, purification
Sage	air/Jupiter	protection, healing, longevity, wisdom
Sagebrush	earth/Venus	visioning, purification
Sunflower	fire/Sun	fertility, healing, wisdom
Tulip	earth/Venus	protection, love, prosperity
Yarrow	water/Venus	courage, love, psychic powers, purification

Brighid's Hot Cocoa

Did we mention that Kristin and Liz are hopelessly addicted to chocolate? This is quite the treat for the chocolate lovers in your life. Red and white are the colors most commonly associated with Brighid. In honor of Her feast day, we offer you a suitable Imbolc twist on the traditional hot chocolate. It is different and delicious!

Materials

- 12 ounces white chocolate
- 2 cups whipping cream
- 6 cups milk
- ½ cup maraschino cherry juice
- ¼ cup granulated sugar
- ½ teaspoon vanilla extract
- 1 tablespoon powdered sugar
- optional: maraschino cherries
- double boiler
- non-metallic stirring spoon

1. Melt white chocolate in top of a double boiler over hot water. Do not allow the water to boil.

2. Combine 1 cup of the whipping cream, milk, 6 tablespoons of the cherry juice, and granulated sugar in a large saucepan. Bring to a boil while stirring. Reduce heat and simmer 3 minutes.

3. Add 1 cup of the mixture from Step 2 to the white chocolate in the double boiler and stir well.

4. Pour the contents of the double boiler into the remaining mixture in the saucepan. Cook over low heat for 6 minutes, stirring often.

5. Beat vanilla and remaining whipping cream with an electric mixer on medium speed until foamy. Gradually add powdered sugar and remaining cherry juice until peaks form.

6. Pour hot chocolate into mugs and spoon on whipped cream mixture. Top with a cherry, if desired.

Buttercream Triskelion Cookies

The triskelion is an ancient symbol commonly used by the Celtic peoples. It embodies the Celtic fascination with threes that represents the three Worlds, the triple deity aspects, the three main phases of life, and much more. These cookies are perfect to serve during Imbolc rituals or a Candlemas feast. We included blackberries as an optional garnish because of their associations with the goddess Brighid. All together, this makes for one mouthwatering delicacy.

Materials

- 1½ cups powdered sugar
- 1 teaspoon cream of tartar
- 1 cup butter
- 1 teaspoon vanilla extract
- 1 teaspoon baking soda
- ¼ teaspoon salt
- 1 egg
- 2¼ cups flour
- mixing spoon or electric mixer
- optional: maraschino cherry juice or blackberries

1. Combine all ingredients except flour and mix well. Add 10–15 drops of cherry juice to make red cookies. If using an electric mixer, use low speed for about 1 minute.

2. Gradually add flour and blend (on low speed with an electric mixer).

3. Chill dough in refrigerator for 20 minutes.

4. Shape dough into ropes, 3–4 inches long.

5. Connect the rope ends to form 3 circles for each cookie. Connect the circles and smooth the central point to help them stick together better. Optional: Place a blackberry in the center of each cookie.

6. Bake at 350° 5–7 minutes and allow to cool before serving.

Traditions From Around the World

The Chinese New Year is a 15-day celebration beginning on the New Moon and ending on the Full Moon. This is a time of honoring the community in any form but particularly family, ancestors, the gods, and pets. This is very much a time of giving thanks and holding to the values of the community. The last day of the celebration is called Lantern Festival, and it is from this festival that we bring you our craft from around the world.

Chinese Lunar Lantern

Each year is governed by one of 12 animals that make up the Chinese horoscope. The animal of the year influences not only those who are born in that year but the year itself. These animals are rat, ox, tiger, rabbit, dragon, snake, horse, sheep, monkey, rooster, dog, and boar. These are favorite images on Chinese lunar lanterns. You may want to use your Chinese animal or some other symbol that is meaningful to you, perhaps the astrological symbol for your Sun or Moon sign.

Chinese Animal	Years	Meanings
Rat	1948, 1960, 1972, 1984, 1996	active, intelligent, ambitious
Ox	1949, 1961, 1973, 1985, 1997	quiet, practical, dependable, honest
Tiger	1950, 1962, 1974, 1986, 1998	positive, adventurous, generous
Rabbit	1951, 1963, 1975, 1987, 1999	sensitive, imaginative, conservative
Dragon	1940, 1952, 1964, 1976, 1988	confident, charismatic, charitable
Snake	1941, 1953, 1965, 1977, 1989	competitive, intellectual, decisive
Horse	1942, 1954, 1966, 1978, 1990	independent, warm, inspired
Sheep	1943, 1955, 1967, 1979, 1991	considerate, spiritual, sensitive
Monkey	1944, 1956, 1968, 1980, 1992	clever, adaptable, friendly
Rooster	1945, 1957, 1969, 1981, 1993	charming, direct, compassionate
Dog	1946, 1958, 1970, 1982, 1994	honest, empathetic, courageous
Boar/Pig	1947, 1959, 1971, 1983, 1995	affectionate, tolerant, friendly

Materials

- printed symbol or design
- poster board: 9" × 7"
- pencil
- scissors
- colored poster board: 9" × 22"
- colored tissue paper
- glue
- craft knife
- embroidery thread

1. Draw or trace your symbol or design onto the 9" × 7" poster board. Using the craft knife, cut this out to create a stencil.

2. Fold the 9" × 22" poster board at 7-inch intervals, forming three panels that each measure 9" × 7", with a 1-inch strip at one end.

3. Place your stencil over each 9" × 7" panel of the folded card and lightly pencil the outline.

4. Cut out the stencil outline, forming the pattern for your lantern. Do not cut along folds.

5. Glue a 6-inch square of tissue paper behind each stencil image.

6. Form the shape of the lantern by gluing the 1-inch strip to the rear 1-inch edge of the last panel.

7. Thread 20-inch lengths of embroidery thread through the top holes in each panel. Tie the thread together and your lantern is ready to hang.

Kid Stuff

For kids, wishing is serious business. There is real magick in the wishes made by a child and belief will help these wishes manifest. Help them to decide on the best wishes for the year to come as they craft these wonderful lanterns.

Wishing Lanterns

These are fun, beautiful, and easy to make, with some adult supervision depending on the age of the child. Liz's 3-year-old had a blast making these little lanterns (with some help) and wanted to make wishes for all of her friends. Make a long string of wishing lanterns as part of a birthday or other celebration. Hang them up and your wishes just might come true!

Materials

- 2 sheets of colored paper
- ruler
- pencil
- scissors
- glue stick
- crayons

1. Cut a piece of paper 6½ inches by 4½ inches.
2. Draw or write your wish on the paper.
3. Roll the paper into a cylinder and glue together at the short ends.
4. Make a handle from a 6½ inch by ½ inch paper strip. Glue it to the top of the cylinder.
5. Select a second piece of paper in a contrasting color and cut a rectangle 6 inches by 6 inches.
6. Fold the paper in half. Cut straight lines from the fold toward the opposite side at ½-inch intervals leaving a ½-inch border.
7. Unfold the cut paper and glue along the border above and below the paper cuts.
8. Attach the border around the top and bottom edge of the cylinder with the central paper fold bulging out around the center of the cylinder.
9. Close your eyes and make your wish. You may want to use a special chant, such as this one:

> *Wishing Lantern, I call on you*
> *Make my hopes and dreams come true.*
> *Wishing Lantern, grant me this*
> *Give to me my every wish.*
> *I wish for_____.*

Chapter 5

Spring Equinox

This first day of spring is always fun and vibrant, no matter what the weather is. In our area of the world, trees and roses are budding out. Many are already in full leaf. Signs of life are everywhere, and baby birds are still resting in their eggs, nearly ready to greet the world.

The Spring Equinox is an astronomical observance. Equinox means "equal night," and on the equinoxes the northern and southern hemispheres of the Earth receive the same amount of sunlight. After the Spring Equinox, days will be longer than nights for people in the northern hemisphere until we reach the Autumn Equinox. So we try to find balance in our world and within ourselves at these times.

Altars and Sacred Space

Spring is a gentle time of fresh air and light colors, when the God and Goddess are young and free, just as the new life on the Earth is. So in this chapter, we bring you sacred space creations that convey balance between God and Goddess and the light feeling of spring breezes.

Serti Silk Altar Cloth

Silk is pure luxury. It is so soft and beautiful and...well, silky. To craft a painted silk altar cloth is to create a thing of true beauty that honors you and any energies or spirits you may work with. In this craft, we show you how to create islands of color on silk—a truly magnificent work of art.

The word *serti* roughly translates as "enclosed," which refers to the way the painted colors are enclosed with a wall of gutta. Gutta is a sticky liquid that prevents the silk paints from spreading across the fabric. Similar to painting by numbers, you fill islands of color that finally come together to create a beautiful image.

Silk dyes act like watercolor paints and will quickly disperse across the fabric. The little island barriers created by the gutta are necessary to maintain a definite image. However, the spreading pigment can also be used to your advantage, blending different colors together to create interesting shading effects. Spots or lines of gutta can also be added to create texture details within an island of color.

There are many silk dyes available. Some require more work than others. We prefer the ones that require steam to set the color because they leave the silk feeling like silk and tend to result in the truest colors. However, there are many good silk dyes that do not require the hassle of steaming.

Traditional gutta is made from latex and can only be removed by dry cleaning. Thankfully gutta-like resists are now available in water-soluble form. (A *resist* is a term used by people who dye or paint fabric; a resist is something that resists the coloring.) If you select a dye that requires steam setting, look for a gutta/resist that is suitable for steaming. But be aware that resists are harder to remove after steaming.

Materials

- pencil
- white paper the same size as your silk cloth
- black marker
- scrap paper
- duct tape
- pushpins
- untreated pure silk cloth
- water-soluble gutta/resist
- applicator bottle with metal tip
- silk paints
- soft art brush
- water
- wood frame (use an old picture frame or construct your own with four lengths of wood cut and nailed together with the same inside dimensions as your silk fabric.)

1. Sketch out your design on a sheet of white paper the same size as your altar cloth. Outline the finished design with black marker.

2. Cover the wood frame with duct tape.

3. Stretch the silk tightly over the wood frame and secure with the pushpins.

4. Place your design directly beneath the framed silk.

5. Trace the outline of your design with the gutta/resist gently squeezed from the applicator bottle directly on to the silk. Practice on scrap paper first.

6. Allow the gutta/resist to dry.

7. Apply a small dab of dye to the center of one shape and gently coax the color toward the outline of the shape with your brush.

8. Repeat Step 7 with each shape. Rinse the brush each time you change dye color.

9. Allow the painted silk to dry.

10. Steam set if applicable (see the next section).

11. Rinse, dry, and enjoy your beautiful altar cloth.

Steam Setting Dyes

Professional silk painters have expensive steam machines for setting dye, but we can make our own with a few kitchen items and some unprinted newsprint.

Materials

- large pasta pot
- vegetable steamer
- netting
- string
- unprinted newsprint
- aluminum foil
- hand towel

1. Create a type of hammock to hold your silk bundle above the steaming water using a vegetable steamer fitted on top of the pot or a piece of netting securely tied around the outer edge of the pan.

2. Lay the dry, painted altar cloth on top of 3 layers of newsprint with a 3-inch border surrounding the silk. Place another 3 layers of newsprint on top of the altar cloth.

3. Roll the sandwiched cloth loosely to form a tube shape. Curl the tube up into a spiral shape and tie with string.

4. Add 3 cups of hot water to the bottom of your pan.

5. Suspend the silk bundle above the water in vegetable steamer or net hammock.

6. Cover the bundle with a dome of aluminum foil. Place a folded hand towel on top of the pan to absorb moisture. Position the pan lid on top of the towel.

7. Bring to the boil then let simmer just below boiling for the appropriate amount of time, usually 30 minutes.

8. Unwrap the hot bundle and hang it out to dry.

Green Man and Spring Maiden Tiles

Decorative tiles can be put together to form a truly magickal tabletop altar. At the Spring Equinox, life is bursting into bud and flower. The energies of the Spring Maiden and Green Man are everywhere, bringing us beautiful colors, renewed vitality, and the innocent beauty of youth. Crafting tiles with the symbols or images of these magickal beings honors the new life around you as it reminds you of the balance brought about by the Equinox.

The history of handcrafted tiles stretches far back in time and across many countries. Anyone wishing to make professional-quality, handcrafted tiles would benefit greatly from taking a class in ceramics. Fortunately, these days we can cheat a little. Many craft stores now sell paints that have been designed for painting on ceramic ware, such as kitchen tiles and plates. Paints vary in application and setting methods, so read all the instructions carefully.

Unless the paint you choose requires heat setting in the oven, you will be able to paint your design directly onto an installed tile. Alternatively, you can paint your tiles and then install them into a mosaic, altar, or frame.

Materials

- 20 glazed, 4-inch white tiles
- ceramic paints: yellow, green, blue, brown
- pencil
- tracing paper
- paintbrush
- carbon paper or cardstock for stencils

1. Sketch or copy an image of the Green Man and an image of the Spring Maiden. The Maiden may be any goddess of springtime, such as Brighid, Niwalen, Eostre, Astarte, or Demeter. Alternatively, you may wish to use symbols of rebirth and balance, such as eggs, a spiral, or the yin/yang symbol.

2. Set out the tiles in 5 rows of 4 tiles.

3. Trace the sketch onto the tiles. You may prefer to use carbon paper or create a stencil by tracing your sketch onto cardstock and cutting out the lines to allow the image to be traced through the holes.

4. Add finishing details and border.

5. Follow the manufacturer's instructions for setting paints.

Suggestions for a Magickal Green Man

- Mix green and blue to make dark green. With a thin brush, paint the outline and veins of all the leaves.

- Mix green and yellow to make light green. Fill in one side of each leaf.

- Use pure green to fill in the other half of each leaf.

- Use pure yellow to fill in the background color.

- Use brown to outline the eyes and lips.

Tools and Oracles

In some areas of the world, young branches are believed to carry a vital life force that can be transferred to people through touch, often by tapping. This early belief may have given rise to the development of the magickal wand. And dowsing rods are a great aid when seeking out life-giving springs of water, or anything you may desire.

Wands

Wand

Let me wave my magick wand and everything will be all right. Don't you wish that were true? It often takes a bit more effort than simply waving your wand, but the creation of a personal wand can be a truly magickal experience.

Wands are used to direct energy. Traditionally, they are crafted from a nutwood or fruitwood (lightning-struck if possible) and measure the distance from your elbow to the tips of your outstretched fingers. But modern wands range from a few inches to several feet in length. We have seen them crafted of glass rods, wooden dowels, driftwood, long crystals, and antlers. The one pictured here was crafted of downed cholla (*pron.* CHOY-ah) cactus. A wand is a very personal object and should reflect you and what is important to you.

You might use yours to cast a spell for money or love. Perhaps you'll use it to clear out negative energy or send love and comfort to a sick friend. You may want one wand for each element to bring you the energies of earth, air, fire, and water. Or maybe it will become a focal point on an altar. Whatever you use it for, it is sure be a beautiful reminder of the magick of life.

Materials

- 1 crystal
- 1 rounded stone
- metal and glass adhesive
- knife, drill, or Dremel tool

- 1 base for your wand: wooden dowel, stick you found on the ground, etc.
- optional decorations: paint, feathers, ribbon, small gemstones, silver or gold wire, beads, shells, colored felt or leather

1. First, plan your wand on a piece of paper. Decide on the colors, symbols, and other materials you want to use. Allow your intuition to guide you. Then be sure to choose a crystal and stone that will fit into (or onto) the ends of your wand.

2. Carve your symbols into the base. You might want to use your astrological sign, a yin/yang, other sacred symbols, or your name in runes.

3. If you are using a wooden base, now is the time to ready it for the crystal, round stone, and any inlaid gemstones you wish you add. Drill or carve an opening in both ends large enough to hold the crystal and round stone. One stone will go in each end. The crystal is the directing end, and the round stone will be your receiving or grounding end. If you have chosen to inlay gemstones, carve a shallow space large enough to hold them.

4. Glue the stones in place and allow to dry completely. Be sure that your wand is supported in such a way that your stones will dry in the correct position. If this is a challenge, you may want to glue one stone at a time.

5. Add any other decorations. Some people like to use colored material around the bottoms of the crystal and stone to give the wand a smoother line. You may want to wrap the wand with wire and glue or tie on beads, feathers, etc.

6. Once your wand is complete and fully dry, take it into a special ritual or sit in meditation with it. Allow your energy to fill the wand and send in any intent you had in its creation. Ask your favorite spirits or deities to bless this wand and any work it may do for the highest good of all concerned. Then find it a special place in your home.

Dowsing Rods

Kristin's son is a whiz with dowsing rods. He makes it look so easy, just as he does with his pendulum. The very first time he picked them up, he had them working perfectly. You might be surprised how many people use dowsing rods—and for all kinds of different reasons. We know people who use them for their traditional use in finding water. We also know people who use them to answer yes and no questions, find lost objects, and even to give an indication of negative energy or electromagnetic fields.

Materials

• pliers	• 1–3 beads large enough to fit snugly over the wire
• tape	• thick wire (copper, silver, etc), approx. 16 inches long and no more than ¼ inch in diameter
• cardstock cut to 7" × 1"	
• pliers	• optional: decorations: paint, markers, ribbon, etc.

1. Bend the copper wire in half at slightly more than a 90-degree angle.

2. Slip 1–3 beads onto the bent end of each wire. Then bend the tip back on itself so the beads do not slip off, approximately ¼ inch in from the tip.

3. Roll the cardstock into tubes. Each tube should fit around one wire as a handle but allow the wire to move freely within it.

4. Fit the tubes over the wires. Bend the bottom ¼ inch of the wire approximately 90 degrees to hold the tubes on.

5. Decorate the tubes as you wish.

Using Your Dowsing Rods

1. First decide on what you will be dowsing for. If you want the answer to a question, make the question very specific and clear before beginning. If you are looking for something, hold a strong image of that object in your mind.

2. Hold one rod in each hand by the handles. Keep them level, and don't begin until they are balanced and still.

3. Holding the question or image in your mind, ask the rods to show you the answer. Feel the energy of your question flow into the rods.

4. If you are asking a question, ask to see your "yes" response first and then your "no" response. Then ask the question and see how the rods move.

5. If you are looking for something, follow the direction the rods point.

Crafts

At the Spring Equinox, we focus on the balance between God and Goddess, but also on the great fun that spring brings. They don't call it Spring Fever for nothing! At this time of year, we all want to enjoy the light pastels of the season and play outside. And that is what the crafts of this chapter are all about.

Goddess and God Flags

As are their Tibetan counterparts, these deity flags are filled with prayers for peace, healing, love, and harmony. A prayer flag is a gift to

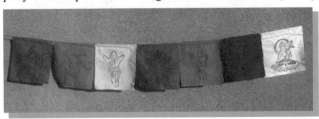

the world delivered by the wind. As your flags fade with the Sun, their messages are released into the universe. When the falling

Prayer flag

flag fibers touch the ground, the earth is blessed. New flags hung along-side old flags remind us of the never-ending circle of life. Good days to hang flags are days of beginnings, such as the day a child is born, birth-days, New Moons, and handfasting or wedding days.

Materials

- tracing paper
- all-natural fiber flag material
- permanent marker
- needle
- scissors
- thread to match your flag material

- 2 images of gods and 2 images of goddesses
- permanent marker
- optional decorations: glitter, beads, paint, etc.
- rope or cord, approximately 6–8 inches longer than the length of your flags laid side by side

1. Trace the deity images or re-create your own interpretation of them on a piece of paper.
2. Cut your material into a flag shape. The most popular shape for a prayer flag is square, but any shape that has a straight top line to hold the string will work well. Triangle, shield, rectangle, and swallowtail shapes all work well. Leave ½ inch of extra material at the top for string attachment.
3. Sew a hem around edge of flag, if you like.
4. Fold the upper hem over to form a tube and sew in place. The string for hanging the flags will go through this tube.
5. Transfer the images onto your flags with permanent marker. Add other decorations as you wish.
6. Thread the finished flags on a length of rope or cord.
7. Knot both ends of the flag string.
8. Hang your flags out in the wind and rejoice as they fade and fray.

Block Printing Flags

Rather than draw or trace your designs directly onto the flags with marker, you might try your hand at block printing. One of the great things about block printing is that you can print the design numerous times. You may decide to use your god and goddess images to make a set of flags or cards for friends.

Block prints are traditionally made from wood or linoleum blocks. Wood offers the added texture of its grain; the linoleum provides a smoother finish. There are various other materials available for block printing. Soft–Kut from Dick Blick Art Supply is exceptionally easy to carve. Remember to always carve away from your body and keep your blades sharp. Keep your carved lines fairly shallow, because deep gouges will weaken the stamp's structure.

Materials

- #2 pencil
- tracing paper
- carbon copy paper
- carving block
- carving tool

- brayer (rubber roller)
- acrylic paint
- sheet of glass (from a picture frame will do)
- flag
- baren or small sponge roller

1. Sketch your design on tracing paper with a soft pencil.
2. Transfer the reverse image onto the carving block by placing the sketch face-down on the carving block and penciling over the back of original pencil lines.
3. Lightly carve the around outline of your design with a small cutting tool.
4. Cut deeper lines with a larger tool.
5. Gouge out the wider areas with a larger tool, leaving only the penciled line design un-carved.
6. Squeeze 1 inch of paint onto the sheet of glass. Then roll your brayer up and down over the paint to make a smooth thin layer of paint on both brayer and glass.
7. Use the loaded brayer to roll an even layer of paint across the surface of the carved block.

    You will now see the reverse image of your design highlighted with the paint.

8. Carve away any excess block that you do not wish to be part of your design.

9. Before printing on a flag practice on a few sheets of paper. Lay the flag or sheet of paper over the painted block. Rub a small dry sponge roller or baren all over the back of the flag.

   Reload the brayer with the paint on glass sheet. Add more paint as needed.

10. Gently peel the flag off the block and lay out to dry.

11. Clean the glass and brayer with mild soapy water once you have finished printing.

Egg Decorations

The potent symbol of the egg can be found in legends of birth and rebirth throughout the world. Blossoming life within the almost circular shell of an egg has long been a part of creation myths. This is a powerful image of transformation, creativity, and fertility.

There are many folk art and religious traditions associated with eggs. To give you a variety of techniques to play with, we offer a few of our favorites. To decide what to include in this book, we made a day of it with friends and children, experimenting with our ideas to come up with some eggceptionally eggcellent eggxamples.

Natural Egg Dyes*

For each of these dyes, boil water (4 quarts will color one dozen eggs) and add the "dye" until the color of the water darkens. You may want to remove the plant material at this point. Add white vinegar (¼ cup to 4 quarts water) and your eggs. Refrigerate overnight and remove the eggs in the morning.

Orange	onion skins (Use more skins for a deeper color.)
Yellow	turmeric
Red	peeled beets or beet juice
Purple	sliced red cabbage: large quantity of inner leaves
Light Blue	sliced red cabbage: small quantity of outer leaves
Brown	use strong coffee in place of the water

*This comes from Kristin Madden's *Pagan Homeschooling* (Spilled Candy Books, 2002).

Egg Blowing

Blowing the yolk and white out of the egg before decorating will enable you to keep your creation without worrying about the egg rotting. This can be done after coloring with natural (or commercial) dyes. This is great fun to do with kids because of the obvious booger jokes that naturally arise during the process.

Materials

- hard-boiled eggs in the egg box
- clean, sharp needle or nail
- paper towels
- 2 bowls: one empty and one full of hot, soapy water

1. With your egg resting in the egg box, use a clean, sharp needle or nail to chip a hole in one end of the egg.
2. Turn the egg over and chip a slightly larger hole in the opposite end of the egg.
3. Poke the needle into the hole and break the membrane of the egg white and yolk.
4. Blow through the small hole, pushing the white and yolk through the larger hole into a bowl.
5. Submerge the empty egg in soapy water, allowing some water to flow in side the egg.
6. Clean the inside of the egg by swirling the water around inside the egg and then blow out the water.
7. Gently pat the egg dry.

NOTE: Egg blowing can make you feel dizzy. If this should happen to you, stop and enlarge the holes before continuing.

Batik

Use hot candle wax to help you create a batik look this year.

1. Splash drips of wax from a burning candle onto your egg before coloring.
2. Dip the waxed egg in cool dye.
3. Remove egg from the dye and peel off the wax to reveal a spotted egg.

Seed and Bead

Small seeds and beads of various colors glued to the outside of an egg make marvelous miniature mosaics. Apple and squash seeds combined with lentils and split peas make nice organic-looking mosaic eggs. Small beads make a more glamorous design. You might like to make a completely freehand design or sketch out a simple outline in pencil first.

Materials

- small seeds and beads
- craft glue
- pin

1. Spread a small amount of ordinary craft glue onto your egg.
2. Using a pin or the tip of your finger, pick up and place each seed or bead on glued area.
3. Allow the egg to dry completely.

Decoupage

Decoupage uses images cut from magazines and wrapping papers that are glued onto an object. When choosing your images, be aware that any image on the back of the page may show through.

Materials

- magazines and wrapping papers
- scissors
- acrylic varnish, polyurethane, or clear nail polish
- craft glue

1. Clean and dry a blown egg.
2. Cut out small images or pieces of colored paper.
3. Glue the cut-out images on to the egg and gently smooth the paper flat with a finger, dispersing any air bubbles.
4. Once the glue is dry, seal the whole egg with a coat of acrylic varnish, polyurethane, or clear nail polish.

Ribbon Threading

Beautifully decorated eggs take on a most luxurious look when threaded on a wide length of ribbon. The ribbon itself will hold the egg in place as it bunches together at each hole.

Before decorating, chip holes into the egg large enough to accommodate the width of ribbon that you have chosen. When decorating is complete, simply thread each egg onto the ribbon.

Fairy Flower Lights

Flower fairy light

These adorable lights are a joy to behold. See three of our favorites here adorning a rock and greenery outside. Let them dance around your living room or brighten up your back yard. They are great fun to make but be sure to read all the safety instructions from the lights you have and use only low-heat bulbs.

Materials

- silk flowers
- florist tape
- silk embroidery thread
- pipe cleaners
- wood beads (20mm)
- black marker
- scissors
- small Christmas tree lights (outdoor/indoor with low heat bulbs)

1. Separate the flower petals from the stems.
2. Cut 3 small slits around the central hole of the flower petals (large enough to slip snugly over the base of the light bulb fitting).
3. Tape the flower petal "skirts" to the bottom edge of the light fitting with florist tape.
4. Fold a pipe cleaner in half and thread it through a "fairy crown" made from one of the cup-shaped plastic parts from the flower.
5. Make fairy hair from 2-inch lengths of silk thread. Lay the center of the hair bundle below the fairy crown and between the fold in the pipe cleaner.
6. Thread the pipe cleaner through a bead to form the fairy's head.

7. Attach the head to the top of the light fitting with the pipe cleaner.

8. Bend the ends of the pipe cleaner to make the fairy's arms.

9. Make the wings from leaves or petals. Then use 3 yards of silk thread folded in half to wrap around the body holding the wings in place and making the top to her dress.

10. Draw the fairy a face with marker pen.

11. Plug in and light up a little fairy magick.

Tie-Dye Cloaks

We love to tie-dye all sorts of stuff but, tie-dye cloaks are some of the neatest things we've seen. The process is great fun but it is rather messy, so be prepared. With some supervision, even children can play with tie-dyeing. Kristin's son makes the best tie-dye shirts around and is constantly improving on his designs.

The application and fixing process of each dye brand varies, so use the same brand of dye for each project. Read the manufacturer's instructions carefully before you start. We recommend using unbleached and untreated 100 percent cotton that has been washed without fabric softener, but you can tie-dye nearly anything. You might try making a tie-dye pointy hat to match your cloak (see Chapter 2).

To find your ideal cloak length, measure from the nape of the neck to the ground, then subtract 4 inches. Cloaks for children only need 45-inch-wide fabric. A full-length adult cloak will require 60-inch-wide fabric.

Materials

- colored chalk
- cotton thread
- needle
- fabric scissors
- string, measuring the ideal cloak length

- pins
- sewing machine (recommended)
- iron (recommended)
- unbleached cotton fabric, measuring twice the ideal cloak length plus 5 inches
- optional: rectangle of fabric 15 inches by 30 inches (see Add a Hood in this chapter)

1. Fold the fabric in half length-wise.

2. Have a friend hold one end of the string stationary at a folded edge corner. With the chalk held at the opposite end of the string, and keeping the string tight, draw a curved line from the folded edge across to the far edge.

3. Cut along the curved line. Do **not** cut along fold line.

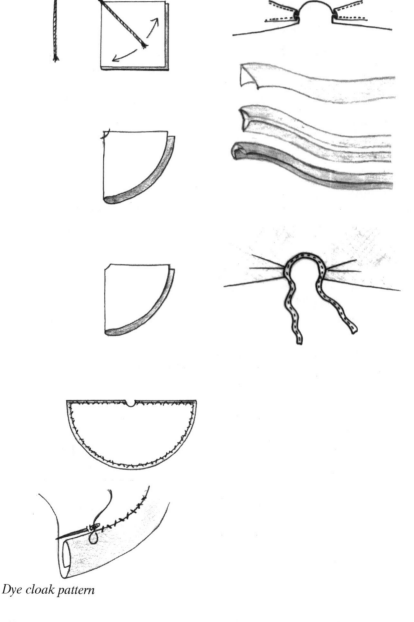

Dye cloak pattern

4. Cut a small curved neck hole close to the fold corner.

5. Sew a hem around sides and bottom edge of the cloak.

6. Fit the cloak across the shoulders and pin a dart or pleat at the top of each shoulder.

7. Cut a 2-inch-by-45-inch strip of material from the leftover fabric.

8. Fold the fabric strip in half, making a 1-inch-wide strip, and iron it flat.

9. Open the strip and fold the long outer edges into the ironed line, running along the center of the strip. Iron these folds flat.

10. Fold the strip in half along the first ironing line, keeping the rough edges tucked in and making a ½-inch strip.

11. Pin the middle of this folded strip around the neck curve. The neck hole should be sandwiched in the middle of the fold and the long ends of the strip will become the cloak ties.

12. Sew the tie along the strip from end to end and along neck.

Add a Hood

1. Cut a rectangle of fabric 15 inches by 30 inches.

2. Fold the fabric in half with right sides together to make a square. Sew from the fold down one side of the square to enclose the back of the hood. Turn the hood right-side out.

3. With right sides together, pin the neck of the hood to the neck of the cloak.

    First, line up the front edges of the hood and cloak necks. Then fold four evenly spaced pleats along the bottom of the hood so that the hood fits perfectly around the neck of the cloak.

4. Stitch a ½-inch seam around the neckline.

5. Sew a hem around the front of the hood as you hem the sides and bottom of the cloak (see Step #5 in the previous section).

6. When you get to Step #11 in the cloak pattern, enclose and sew the raw edges of the neckline in the fabric strip as described. Then lay the bulky neckline flat against the cloak and sew it in place, leaving the ends of the tie loose for tying.

When tie-dying, keep in mind that colors change when mixed together. Complementary colors that work well together are red and yellow, yellow and blue, and blue and red. When mixed, they produce new colors. For example, yellow and red mixed make orange. This reduces the need for a special orange, green, or purple dye and allows you to be even more creative with your designs. Try the suggestions that follow or come up with your own.

Crystal Clouds

This process gives the appearance of clouds of crystalline color wafting across your cloak or shirt.

Materials

- cloak, t-shirt, etc.
- 2 squeeze bottles
- 2 dye colors
- string

1. Lay the material out flat.
2. Starting at the center and working around in a spiral, gather the cloak toward the center in small bunches, until the whole cloak is scrunched up into a large wheel.
3. Tie with string.
4. Squirt splotches of dye color all over the cloak.
5. Fix dye according to the manufacturer's directions.
6. Rinse, untie, and dry.

Wings of Color

Kristin's son calls this the Eagle Feather design because it reminds him of eagle feathers around his neck and shoulders. It can be a very striking design. The half-circle cloak above works perfectly for this rainbow tie-dye design. Alternating two of the complementary colors down the length of the cloak will give you a more harmonious effect. Remember to let the colors bleed together at the edges.

Materials

- cotton cloak
- 3 squeeze bottles
- fabric dye: red, yellow, and blue
- string or rubber bands

1. Starting at one front seam, pleat your cloak in wedge-shaped folds until your whole cloak resembles a large closed paper fan.

2. Use rubber bands or lengths of string to tie knots around the closed fan shape of your cloak. Space the bands or knots about 3 inches apart at the top of the cloak and gradually increase the distance to about 6 inches apart at the bottom of the cloak.

3. Prepare dye according to manufacturer's instructions.

4. Fill squeeze bottles with dye. Squirt dye into the folds and creases of the fabric.

 Start with the color red at the bottom ⅓ of the cloak.

5. Squirt yellow so that it overlaps some of the red and continues to ⅔ of the way up the cloak.

6. Add blue, overlapping some of the yellow and continuing to the top of the cloak.

7. Add a circle of red dye at the top of the cloak.

8. Follow the manufacturer's instructions for fixing the dye.

9. Rinse, untie, dry, and enjoy.

Magickal Delicacies

This is the feast day of Eostre, the Saxon fertility goddess, and the Christian holiday celebrated around this time bears a striking resemblance to her name. Eggs were sacred to Eostre and are a common element of this time of year. Another common element of this time of year is allergy season. So with both of those ideas in mind, we bring you these magickal delicacies.

Egg Custard

One of Kristin's earliest and most wonderful memories is that of her maternal grandmother making egg custard. The entire kitchen smelled of nutmeg and butter. She served it warm in thick, dark brown cups and bowls. The creamy sweetness would just melt in the mouth. Though yours may not evoke the same memories, you can enjoy the same silky smoothness and not-too-sweet taste without slaving in the kitchen all day.

Materials		
• 3 egg yolks	• 1½ cups heavy cream	• double boiler
• ¼ cup sugar	• 1 teaspoon vanilla extract	• small bowl
	• wire whisk	

1. Beat egg yolks, sugar, 1 cup cream, and vanilla in a double boiler.
2. Cook on high until thick, beating continually.
3. Remove from heat. Continue beating until cool.
4. Whip ½ cup cream until soft peaks form and gently fold into custard.
5. Refrigerate for at least 1 hour before serving.

Allergy-Buster Tea

For many people, this is also a time for allergies. Everything is pollinating and allergens are everywhere, making our noses run and our eyes itch and resulting in terrible sneezing fits at the most inappropriate times. This tea is delicious and effective. It works wonders for Kristin's son every spring.

Materials

• dried herbs: choose as many or as few of these as you like for your tea

Peppermint (*Mentha piperita*)	soothing to the mucus membranes; also thins mucus
Blackberry leaf (*Rubus* spp.)	excellent tonic for mucus membranes; specific for post-nasal drip
Licorice (*Glycyrrhiza glabra*) or Marshmallow (*Althaea officinalis*)	soothing to the mucus membranes; also thins mucus
Perilla leaf (*Perilla frutescens*)	reduces congestion and cough
Elder flowers (*Sambucus nigra*)	reduces congestion
Hyssop leaves (*Hyssopus officinalus*)	reduces congestion and cough; expectorant
Honeysuckle flowers (*Lonicera japonica* or *caprifolium*)	soothes sore throats and swollen eyes or itchy eyes

• local honey (The pollen contained in local honey can act homeopathically, reducing allergic reactions to local pollen.)

• small muslin tea bag or tea ball (preferably stainless steel)

• your favorite mug

1. Place equal amounts of each herb in your tea ball.

2. Heat water to boiling. Fill mug ½ to ¾ full with boiling water and place tea ball in to steep.

3. Allow to steep for 10 minutes. Add ½–1 teaspoon of honey to your taste.

4. Enjoy—preferably without milk (which increases mucus production).

Traditions From Around the World

Meaning "new day," Naw-Ruz is the Baha'i and Iranian new year, occurring on or near the date of the Spring Equinox. This is a time of feasting and renewing the bonds of community as well as our spiritual connections to the Divine. It is celebrated with various symbols associated with spring and renewal. This is a time rich in tradition and meaning. Two of our favorite aspects of Naw-Ruz are the symbolic feast and a purification ritual. We have adapted these, with great respect for their origins, to present to you for your spring celebrations.

The Magickal Feast

In honor of the Spring Equinox, the returning of life to our lands, and the balance of light and dark, invite your loved ones to a magickal feast. The traditional Naw-Ruz feast table is set with fruit, cakes, colored eggs, a holy book, and a mirror. You may prefer to set yours with symbols of your spirituality and crafts that you have created specifically for this holiday.

Allow the sprouted lentils a special place at the table. Dedicate the first toast to the spirits of these plants as well as to yourselves for freely releasing your unwanted energies and patterns. After that, focus your discussions, toasts, and attention to all the wonderful things you are creating in your lives and your community.

Lentil Purification

1. Place fresh, dry lentils into a dish of water.

2. Leave them in the Sun and keep moist so that they sprout. This should take a few days to a week.

3. The day of your feast, allow each person time to send any energies they wish to be cleared of into the sprouted lentils. Ask these new plants to help you transform these energies into a creative force within you.

4. After the feast, throw the lentils into running water to carry away and cleanse the energies. If you do not live near a stream or river, you may choose to bury them to allow the Earth to transform these energies into new life.

Kid Stuff

Ask just about any little one and he or she will tell you that spring is fairy season! Fairies care for Nature and bring beautiful blessings to those they love. What better way to honor the fairies that live in your area, and encourage them to stay nearby, than to build a house just for them?

Fairy House

When building a fairy house it is important to find an enchanting, peaceful space in Nature. Try to find a place that feels right. Whether you build a small shelter among the flowers of a window box or a fairy castle of entwined twigs in the forest, you can build a special place for your fairy friends. The natural habitat where you live will greatly influence the materials used for the construction of your fairy house.

First find a private, pretty spot to build your fairy house: A bed of flowers, an herb garden, a mound of grass, beneath an attractive tree or bush, and a rocky ledge with a nice view are all good fairy house places. A beach or riverfront fairy house must be built well away from the tide line. Build your fairy house in a safe, sheltered place not far from the ground and away from prickly plants and steep ledges.

Fairies like to live in environmentally friendly houses, so choose natural building materials without harming Nature in any way. Use fallen leaves and downed branches rather than picked leaves and living branches. It is okay to use the freshly cut branches, vines, and grasses from plants that benefit from being trimmed.

Begin by building a basic frame from small branches. Then fill in the walls and roof with twigs or leaves and grasses. If the soil is soft, push part of each frame branch into the ground to make a stable foundation for your fairy house. Vines and long blades of grass, straw or even a few strands of long hair make good string for tying things together. Sticky mud makes marvelous glue. Look around and see what treasures you can find: rocks, pebbles, shells, acorns, pinecones, nut husks, tree bark, cacti skeletons, feathers, straw, tufts of wool, drift wood, sand dollars, seaweed, bamboo, fern, fossils, and seed pods—all these and many more are Nature's treasures and will help make a beautiful fairy home.

If you still have snow and ice on the ground, you can make a snow cave for your fairy friends. Then build them a new house in the summer.

If finding natural treasures is a challenge where you live, you can still build an environmentally friendly fairy home by recycling some clean trash. A shoe box, cereal box, kitchen roll tube, and fabric scraps will work quite well. Keep this fairy house at home, perhaps on a windowsill or balcony.

With a little imagination, you can build a fine fairy castle, maybe even give them some furniture too. Fairies love to dance so, if you can, give them a circle of stones or plant some flowers for them to dance around.

Chapter 6

Beltane

B eltane takes its name from the Celtic Sun god Bel and means Bel's Fire or the Good Fire. As such, it is the time of the great balefires or bonfires. In ancient Ireland, cattle were passed between two balefires to increase fertility and magickally protect them from disease. Couples would pass between or jump the fires to increase their chances of having children. Many people today still jump the fires or dance the Maypole for fertility and good fortune.

As the time of the great marriage between god and goddess, Beltane may be best known as a fertility festival, but it is great fun for all ages. Communities around the world come together for planting and tending to the fields. This second of the spring festivals is the time of year when Nature is in full bloom. The richness and diversity of life on this Earth is evident everywhere you look. Vibrant colors and the appearance of young wildlife only add to the feeling of excitement as we celebrate the last of the spring festivals in unabashed joy and passion for life.

Altars and Sacred Space

Our sacred space offerings for this chapter are steeped in history and tradition, as Beltane itself is. A traditional altar brings through the energy of hundreds, if not thousands, of years of focused attention and use. And of course, the Maypole is **the** symbol of this festival.

Traditional Altar

A traditional altar is fairly formal and most often occupies a special table all its own. Though each spiritual path has its own unique symbols and locations for ritual elements, a personal or family altar often works best when you allow it to develop and change naturally. The creation of an altar allows your own magickal creativity to come through as you tune in to spirit guidance. In order to jumpstart that flow, we offer you some basic guidelines for the development of an altar. Use these recommendations as a base from which to start, and adjust whatever you feel is right for you.

Materials

- table

- matches

- incense or smudge

- fireproof container

- candles: at least one central altar candle plus candles for deities, protection, candle spells, etc. as you desire

- symbols representing your spirit guides, deities, your path, the elements, and anything else you hold sacred

- ritual tools: ritual dagger, rattle, wand, runes, etc.

1. Begin with a plan for your altar.

   Most altars have a beautiful cloth as their foundation. There are many varieties of altar cloths in this book that you can make yourself or you might already have the perfect piece of material for your altar. You may even prefer to use something with sentimental value: a doily embroidered by your great-grandmother or a piece of your very first cloak or ritual robe, for example.

   Many traditions associate an element or animal with each direction and place symbols of these at those points on the altar. These associations vary, and you might choose a beautiful feather or bubble wand to represent air at the east, a candle or small dragon statue to symbolize fire at the south, a cup of water or a seashell to bring through water in the west, or a bowl of earth or a stone as the earth in the north.

   Some traditions have one candle for the Goddess (often silver or in female form) and one for the God (often gold or in the male form). Others simply have one large white altar candle in the center.

Ritual or meditative tools are often kept on the altar. Incense, crystals, ritual daggers, rattles, and smudge fans are common ritual elements.

Anything that holds or represents spirituality and your path for you should rightly be placed in the most sacred place: your altar. These may include locks of hair, power pouches, jewelry, photos or drawings, twigs, or even pieces of plants.

2. Place your altar items according to your plan and see how it feels. Would something feel or look better in another place, or do you have an idea of an item that might replace one of the originals you considered? Go with how you feel and keep playing with it. You will get it right—and when you do, the energy will flow smoothly and beautifully, making for easier meditations and other ritual work.

Maypole

The Maypole is one of the most obvious of human fertility rituals. Each May Day, people around the world erect a large solid pole into a hole, top it with a circle of flowing ribbons then dance merrily all around. How wonderful that this saucy May ritual is still around after all these years!

This frolic around the Maypoles of the world is symbolic not only of the union of god and goddess but also of the fruitful fertility of the land, the people, and all the animals on earth. A child that was conceived in the merry mating of these fertile celebrations was "merry begot," believed to be a child of the gods.

The construction of the Maypole is all part of this wonderful celebration. The choosing of the tree, the blessing of the hole, the erecting of the pole, the dance and the taking down of the Maypole—each step is a part of this beautiful journey. Traditionally men craft the shaft and women make the ribbon ring and prepare the hole.

The first step in Maypole making is to select the pole. In the past, Maypoles were made from a perfect tree found in the woods. Today, this option is often not possible, and some people have ethical concerns with cutting a live tree. Fortunately, there are options. You can find a fine pole in your local lumberyard. You might also consider using an old flagpole or beam, wooden or otherwise.

Materials	
• sandpaper	• tacks or staple gun
• wood oil	• decorations: paint or wood-burning tools
• 6-inch wooden disk	
• 15-feet-long ribbons (one for each person)	• drill with ¼-inch bit and screws
	• shovel
• pencil	• sacred herbs, such as lavender or sagebrush
• a pole: 12 feet long and 6 inches around	
	• pure water

Preparing the Pole

1. Sand the pole until smooth.
2. Decorate your pole with symbols and words or simply oil it well.

The Ring of Ribbons

1. Drill a hole in the center of the wooden disk.
2. With the pencil, mark the placement of the ribbons evenly around the top of the disk.
3. Attach the end of each ribbon to the center of the disk and lay them across the top of the disk. Use several small tacks or a staple gun to hold each ribbon firmly in place.
4. Drill a ¼-inch hole in to the top of the pole.
5. Screw the center of the disk to the top of the pole.

Preparing and Erecting the Hole

1. Dig a 1-foot-deep hole.
2. Bless the hole with sacred herbs and pure water.
3. Plant the bottom end of the pole firmly in the ground.

   NOTE: Alternatively, erect the pole in a sturdy patio umbrella stand.

Dancing the Maypole

Dancing the Maypole is great fun, even more so as you learn the traditional steps to the dance. This is wonderful when accompanied by chanting, drumming, or Celtic music. To do the traditional dance, each person holds the end of a ribbon, several paces out from the Maypole so that the ribbon is taut.

Have the group count off from 1 to 2. Number Ones face clockwise, and Number Twos face counterclockwise. Start slowly with Number Ones walking clockwise and lifting their ribbons high. Number Twos travel counterclockwise and duck under the ribbons of the Number Ones.

Once past the first person, they switch: The Number Twos continue counterclockwise but hold their ribbons up high to allow the Number Ones walking clockwise to duck under the Number Twos' ribbons. Continue to go over and under, skipping and dancing, until all the ribbon has been woven down the length of the pole. Tie the ends of the ribbons to secure your weaving.

When the dance is all done, the Maypole is usually left up until the end of the celebrations. Take it down as part of a closing ritual and store it somewhere safe and dry until next year.

Some people unravel the ribbons for reuse in a new dance the next year. Others prefer to remove the weaving and keep it in a special place for fertility blessings throughout the year.

The following chant is said while dancing the Maypole:

Traditional English Rhyme

Dancing round the maypole, dancing all the day,
Dancing round the maypole, on the first of May.
Dancing round the maypole, what a merry bunch,
Dancing round the maypole, till it's time for lunch.
Dancing round the maypole, shouting out with glee,
Dancing round the maypole, till it's time for tea.
Dancing round the maypole, blue and white and red,
Dancing round the maypole, till it's time for bed.

Tools and Oracles

Though most people perceive Samhain, or Halloween, as the time of year when the Veil between world is the thinnest, there are some traditions that believe that this thinning of the Veil also occurs at Beltane. In some areas of the British Isles, a door was said to open into the land of Faery on this date. As a result, this is an ideal time to work not only with fertility but also with divination and spirit allies.

Dream Diary

Dreaming is powerful magick. In dreaming, all things are possible. When you learn to consciously work with dreaming, you open a doorway to self-knowledge, inspiration, and more. Of course, all of this takes practice, and the best way to begin is to simply record your dreams.

The creation of a dream diary is a fantastic way to start on a journey of connection and working with spirit guides. A dream diary can help you work through challenges, find answers to problems, and gain insight into life situations. Children have great fun telling and recording their dreams. They seem to innately know the power of dreaming. To encourage them to keep a dream diary can prevent them from blocking their natural psychic abilities and trust in themselves.

Of course, you can purchase elaborate or plain blank books in nearly any bookstore these days, but why not consider enhancing your personal dream diary with your own energy by crafting a dream diary cover? This really does have a way of making your dream diary a sacred and special object that is just for you.

Materials

- cotton fabric
- diary or journal
- cotton thread
- tape measure
- pins
- double-fold bias tape or quilt binding
- beads
- scissors
- thin ribbon
- needle
- optional: sewing machine

1. Open your diary and lay the sides flat. Measure all around it as one rectangular shape.

2. Cut a rectangle of material 1 inch longer and 1 inch wider than the book measurement.

3. Cut two strips of material the same length from top to bottom as the previously cut rectangle but only 3 inches wide.

4. Cut two lengths of bias tape the same length as the strips of material. Place one edge of each strip in the center fold of the bias tape. Pin and sew the tape in place.

5. With wrong sides together, pin the 3-inch strips to the outer edges of the book sleeve with the bias tape toward the center.

6. Frame the whole book sleeve with a border of bias tape pinned in place. Sew in place.

7. To add a bookmark, cut a length of thin ribbon 4 inches longer than the length of the diary. Tie a knot in one end, add a few beads, and knot the other end before sewing it to the center, top edge of the diary cover.

Flower Petal Covers

Flowers are one the most beautiful things of this time of year. We love to see a display of colorful roses and their scent is simply divine. Petal printing is a wonderful way of permanently preserving a little of that beauty. In the spirit of Beltane, you might try this for your dream diary cover or for a dream pillow (see later in this chapter).

Materials

- unbleached muslin
- freshly picked colorful flowers
- contact paper
- magazine
- rubber mallet

1. Cut out your dream diary cover pattern from unbleached muslin.

2. Collect a handful of richly colored flower petals. Velvety-textured flowers such as deep red roses work well.

3. Arrange the petals in concentric circles on the top side of the fabric.

4. Cover the completed arrangement with contact paper, press the petals firmly in place on the fabric.

5. Place the material face up over a magazine.

6. Firmly bash down on each petal repeatedly with the flat end of a rubber mallet.

7. When you are sure you have squeezed all of the juicy flower pigment into the fabric, gently remove the contact paper and crumpled petals.

8. Follow the previous directions to turn your petal-printed fabric into a dream diary cover using bias tape of a contrasting color.

Leaf Printing

If bashing pretty petals with a hammer feels barbaric, try the gentle art of leaf printing instead.

Materials

- nicely shaped leaves
- tubes of gouache paints
- plate or artist's palette
- newsprint or scrap paper
- wedge shaped cosmetic sponge
- dream pillow and diary cover

1. Select green and yellow paints for spring leaves or red and orange paints for an autumnal look. Squeeze a little of each color onto a plate or pallette.

2. Pat the sponge in the paint and dab a leaf with patches of color, covering one side of the leaf completely with paint.

3. Place the painted side of the leaf down on the fabric. Cover with newsprint or a scrap of clean paper and use your hand to press down firmly on the leaf.

4. Gently remove paper and leaf to reveal your lovely leaf print.

Dream Pillow

These little bow-tied dream pillows are simple to make and easy to

Dream diary and pillow

refresh with new herbs or a few drops of pure essential oil. With a bit of thought, you can use this pillow to help you direct your dreaming or create a particularly restful night of sleep. Place your dream pillow beneath your bed pillow throughout the day. Before you go to sleep, turn your bed pillow over so that your head rests on the fragrant side.

Materials

- rectangle of cotton material: 12" × 9"
- 38" of double fold bias tape
- cotton thread
- needle
- optional: sewing machine
- cotton ball
- 1 cup of dream herbs (see page 101 for special mixtures)

1. Sew a bias tape hem along the top 12-inch edge of the cotton material.
2. With right sides together, fold the material in half with the two 9-inch sides together.
3. Sew together along the side and bottom. Turn the pouch right-side out.
4. Stuff the pillow with one cup of dreaming herbs and top with a cotton ball.
5. Cut a 26-inch length of bias tape. Unfold the tape and tie into a decorative bow around the stuffed pillow.

Dreaming Herbs

Growing and drying your own herbs and flowers for your dream pillow will add added energy to your home and your dreaming but you can make a perfectly good dream pillow with store-bought herbs and flowers.

Dreaming takes place in the REM cycle of sleep, not a deep sleep cycle. For this reason, it is important not to overload your dream pillow with too much sleeping potion. It is preferable to use a mild sedative herb in combination with a preferential scent and stimulant. Select your own combination of herbs or follow one of these magickal combinations.

Peaceful dreaming	Lavender, rose, and chamomile. Add lemon balm for a more refreshing scent.
Vision dreaming	Lavender, passionflower, and valerian with a dash of nutmeg.
Passion dreaming	Fresh rose petals and dried jasmine flowers with a few drops of sandalwood pure essential oil.
Joyful dreaming	Mullein, lemon balm, and elderflower.

Interpreting Dreams

Sometimes dreams make perfect sense. Other times they are just too weird for words and you are left scratching your head, wondering what the heck that dream meant. Books on the meanings of dream images can be good places to get ideas and start the intuitive juices flowing.

But you can begin to develop your own dream symbol reference by keeping a dream diary. Keep track of the symbols. When you believe you have a meaning for them, note that in your diary. Over time, your personal symbolic reference will be much more valuable for you than any reference book you can find in a store.

Begin a dialogue with each symbol or imagine you have become each one separately. How does it feel? What would it say in the context it has appeared? This will give you clues to what your mind associates with each symbol and what they might mean in the context of the other symbols they appear with.

You can also begin to interpret your dreams by breaking them down and then building them back up. Using an association web (see the next paragraph), brainstorm your associations for each individual component then for each combination of components. Then do the same for each scene and the dream as a whole. Be sure to note how each element makes you feel and any memories or ideas that spring to mind when you consider it.

In an association web, you start with a root word. Perhaps you dreamed of a mouse with wings sitting on the Moon. Your root word may be mouse, wings, Moon, or even sitting. Write that word in the center of a clean sheet of paper. Now write down everything that this root word brings up for you. The word wings may give rise to flight, fairy, rising above, escape, success, and so on. Write these new words out from the root word and connect them with lines. If those new words bring up additional words, "web" them as well. Here's a sample web:

```
            escape        rising above this
                 \       /
magick — fairy — WINGS — flight — travel — journeying
                 /       \
            success        bird spirits — inspiration
```

Crafts

As with the Beltane fairs of old, our craft offerings for this section are diverse, though they all relate to the elements of the season. These crafts evoke the bonds of family, the pleasure of intimacy, God and Goddess, and the flowering Earth.

Massage Oil

Beltane is such a sensual time, full of intimacy and physical pleasure. This is great time to get or give a massage. There need not be anything sexual about it, just allow yourself to give and receive physical intimacy with someone you trust. This relaxes you as it gets your energy flowing and brings a beautiful glow to your entire being.

Materials

- 6 teaspoons extra virgin or cold pressed oil: olive, sesame, peanut, grapeseed, safflower, or sunflower
- 9 drops essential oils

1. Blend oils together well. For a nice Beltane balance, try mixing musk with jasmine or patchouli with lavender.
2. Pour into brown or cobalt glass bottles and seal tightly. Keep in a dark, cool place out of the reach of children.
3. Warm slightly before using.

Lavender Wand

Lavender may well be the high priestess of flowering shrubs! This long, slender plant with its purple blossoms and sumptuous aroma has the ability to bring balance to mind and body. Called by many the "herb of love," lavender's aphrodisiac properties are used in many love potions. You may want to hang this wand in your bedroom to enhance that loving feeling. Although a lavender wand is not used in the same way as a traditional magickal wand, there is no doubt that this little bundle of blossoms will spread some very powerful magick through your home.

Materials

- 13 long stems of fresh lavender
- 3 yards of thin purple ribbon

1. Cut 13 long stems of lavender at dawn, just before the flowers open to capture the best aroma.
2. Bunch the lavender together and tightly tie a knot around the base of the flowers with ribbon. Leave one (short) end of the ribbon 21 inches long.

3. Bend each stem backwards just below the knot, so that it lays over the flower heads. When all 13 stems are bent over, the flower heads will be enclosed in an umbrella pattern of stems.

4. Keep the long ribbon at the top of the umbrella and let the short 21-inch ribbon end hang down beside the stems.

5. Moving clockwise, weave the long ribbon in and out of the stems. Under one over the next continually, tightly enclosing the flowers in a spiral cocoon.

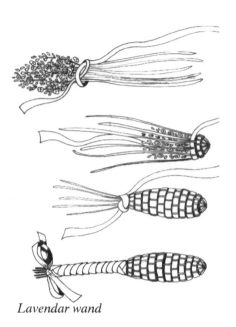

Lavendar wand

6. Once the flowers have been completely enclosed, tie the two ribbon ends together at the base of the lavender cocoon.

7. Spiral the remaining ribbon down the length of the lavender stems.

8. Fasten the ribbon ends into a bow or loop for hanging.

Stag Mask

The stag plays a leading role in many Beltane traditions. He is the Horned God who chases and eventually seduces the Goddess. He embodies the strength and virility of the God. The image of a stag is a powerful way to invoke this energy, connecting us with the beauty of the Sacred Marriage and the abundance of creative fertility that this season brings. Mask making connects us with our shamanic origins. Crafting a stag mask allows us to shapeshift, merging with the fertile energy of the Horned God.

That's Kristin's son behind the stag mask on the cover of this book. Notice that Liz used fallen branches for the antlers on that mask. You can try molted antlers but, unless they are small ones, they are likely to be too heavy for this mask.

Materials

- scissors
- glue
- pencil
- duct tape
- paint
- paintbrushes

- fallen branches that resemble stag's antlers
- cardboard box slightly larger than your face
- dowel (approx. 1½ feet long) to use as a handle for the mask

1. Cut a face from the corner of a cardboard box. Make the face an upside-down pear or diamond shape with the corner fold of the box running down its center.

2. Cut two large leaf-shapes with the corner of the box running down the center of each to form the stag's ears.

3. Snip a ½-inch slit from the bottom of each ear along the center fold. Overlap the bottom edges of each ear and glue them together to form a concave ear shape.

4. Glue the bottom edges of the ears onto the mask.

5. Sketch the shape of the stag's eyes and cut a hole in the center of each eye.

6. Cut two half-moon shapes from the cardboard to form eyelids.

7. Bend the eyelid shapes slightly so that they protrude from the stag's face. Glue the eyelids into place.

8. Cut out a nose and glue it into place.

9. Tape the antler branches to the back of the mask.

10. Tape the dowel to the back of the chin of the mask so that it forms a handle below the stag's face.

11. Paint the face. Be sure to paint the back side of the mask to cover the duct tape.

Banner

Banners are a great way to show off your coven, grove, or family identity at gatherings. Banners can also be made for any celebration. How about making a "Welcome to this World" banner for a new baby or a "Congratulations!" for the new graduate in your life? Banners are equally wonderful when you want to convey a special message such as "World Peace" or "Gay Pride."

Materials

- pencil
- paper
- tracing paper
- selection of colored felt
- fabric glue
- needle and thread
- scissors
- pins
- 2 curtain rod ends or 2-inch wooden balls
- cord
- 1-inch dowel or curtain rod that is 2 inches longer than the top edge of the banner

1. Sketch out your banner design. Most banners are basic rectangles in shape. The bottom edge of the banner may be straight or curved, swallowtail, or shield shaped, but the top edge should remain straight for ease of hanging.

2. Break the image down into simple-shaped blocks of color.

3. Once your basic sketch is finished, draw your banner to scale on a large sheet of paper. Number each shape for easy reference.

4. Trace each shape onto a piece of tracing paper and write down the reference number and color.

5. Cut out all the traced pieces to use as a pattern. Separate the pattern pieces by color.

6. Arrange the pattern pieces on the selected color of felt. Pin into place and cut out each shape. Before cutting out the banner's background shape, allow an extra 5 inches of material at the top.

7. Fold the top 4 inches of extra background felt over to form the tube that holds the dowel. Sew a hem along the bottom edge of the folded tube.

8. Use the reference numbers to arrange the felt pieces. Glue or pin and sew each piece into place on the banner's background.

9. Slide the dowel into the top tube. Attach the curtain rod ends or glue a wooden ball to each end of the dowel.

10. Tie the hanging cord or ribbon to each end of the dowel.

Magickal Delicacies

It should come as no surprise that the recipes we offer you for Beltane are sensual and sinfully good. At Beltane, life is far too good not to enjoy luscious delights. These sumptuous delicacies will make you and your friends all feel like kings and queens of the May!

May Wine

May wine or punch is an old and well-loved custom for May Day. Traditionally, it was made with Sweet Woodruff (*Galium odoratum*). In some herbal references, this is referred to as *Asperula odorata*. Woodruff has beautiful little white flowers that bloom on or near May Day. It has many medicinal properties. It has also been said to act as a strong sedative, though we can find no clinical proof of this.

Materials

- 8–10 clean, green sprigs of fresh woodruff
- 1½ cups sugar
- 1 bottle Rhine wine or other dry to semi-sweet wine, preferably white
- ice
- punch bowl
- 12 fresh, ripe strawberries

---

1. In a large bowl, combine woodruff, sugar, and bottle of wine.

2. Cover, and refrigerate for no more than 24 hours. Steeping longer tends to create a bitter result.

3. Remove the cover, stir, and remove the woodruff.

4. Pour the wine over ice in a punch bowl. Add strawberries and serve.

Strawberries With Whipped Cream and Melted Chocolate

Few desserts speak to the sensuality of Beltane the way strawberries and cream do. This is a wonderfully fresh and fun dessert. It is made even better with homemade whipped cream, which is so much easier to make than we once believed. As an added pleasure, we like to dip our strawberries first into the melted chocolate, then into the whipped cream, then into our happy, by-now-salivating mouths. Adults may want to add the optional dark rum or Marsala wine to the melting chocolate.

Materials

- 6 ounces milk or dark chocolate
- ½ cup heavy whipping cream
- pure vanilla extract
- sugar
- electric mixer
- small saucepan
- spoon
- optional: ½ tablespoon dark rum or Marsala wine
- ½ pound fresh, ripe strawberries
- small mixing bowl

1. Melt the chocolate with 1 teaspoon heavy cream in a small saucepan over medium-low heat. (If you are adding rum or wine, add ½ teaspoon cream and ½ tablespoon alcohol.)

2. Stir constantly until melted and mixed well. Remove from heat and keep warm.

3. Combine the remaining cream, vanilla extract, and sugar in a small mixing bowl.

4. Mix on high until stiff peaks begin to form in the cream.

5. Dip and enjoy!

Traditions From Around the World

Floralia was a Roman festival honoring Flora, goddess of flowers. The festival was intended to please Flora and encourage her to protect the beautiful blossoms that graced the land at this time of year. Known later on as the Ludi Florales, this was a time of theatre and games.

Flower Crown

It was common for the people to wear crowns or wreaths of flowers during the Floralia, much as we see today at May Day celebrations around the world. May queens and princesses of all ages love the simple beauty and feminine feeling of wearing these flower crowns. Liz's daughter Rhianna graces the cover of this book wearing her beautiful flower crown.

Materials

- green stem wire
- green florist stem tape
- green florist reel wire
- silk or dried flowers with leaves
- thin ribbon
- optional: pliers

1. Twist two or three stem wires together, to form a single length of wire 2 inches longer than the circumference of your head. Cover with florist tape. This will form the base of your crown.
2. Bend a small loop at one end of the length of wire.
3. Join little bunches of flowers and leaves together with reel wire.
4. Lay the first bunch over the loop end of the crown and tie the stems into place with green reel wire.
5. Cover the reel wire with a small amount of florist tape.
6. One at a time, tie each bunch into place along the length of the crown. Overlap each bunch of flowers to hide the stems of the previous bunch. Cover all but the last inch of crown wire with little bunches of flowers.
7. Bending the crown into a circle, hook the last inch of wire through the loop end of the crown and tighten it to be comfortable.
8. Tie long lengths of thin ribbon to the back of your flower crown.

Kid Stuff

With lively music and vivid colors adorning people and the Earth, Beltane is a great time to let loose and make noise. Kids of all ages can have plenty of fun using rattles for music, ritual, or just making noise. Noise and music can be fabulous ways of expressing and releasing emotions. This can be particularly valuable for young children who are still learning to understand and handle their emotions. As with all our kids' crafts, this is a fairly simple project, but it does require adult supervision and a bit of adult help using sharp objects.

Gourd Rattle

Since ancient times, gourds have been used to create rattles, bowls, and even water dippers. As largely round fruits of the Earth containing seeds, gourd rattles embody the union of God and Goddess. Through their marriage, beautiful music is brought forth and wonderful things manifest themselves.

Materials

- small to medium-sized gourd
- strong knife or small saw
- sandpaper
- 1 teaspoon–1 tablespoon dried seeds
- craft glue
- stick or dowel at least 10 inches long
- 4-inch or longer leather or cloth strip
- pencil and paper
- optional decorations: leather, fabric, glitter, feathers, beads, etc.

1. You may want to purchase a dried gourd for this project. But you can get a fresh gourd, cut it into the right size and shape for your rattle, hollow out the seeds and flesh, and let it dry completely. This can take anywhere from 1 week to 1 month. Once dry, the colors of the gourd will be paler but the skin is perfect for drawing or carving.

    Either way, be sure to cut the gourd below the fat, round part, leaving a small bit (1–2 inches) of the narrow part to hold your handle. Obviously, an adult will need to do the cutting and let the kids do the rest.

2. Once the gourd is cut and dry, roll up a piece of sandpaper and smooth out the inside where the handle will go. You want to make an opening large enough to fit the stick or dowel for your handle.

3. Plan the rattle design on a piece of scrap paper. Have the kids decide what images and symbols they want on their rattles, what colors they might want to paint them, and what other decorations they would like to add.

4. If you plan to paint the surface of the gourd, do that now and allow the paint to dry completely before proceeding.

5. Inscribe your name or magickal symbols on the gourd.

6. Place a small amount of dried beans or seeds inside the gourd. With a finger over the opening, test the sound. Add or remove seeds until the sound is right. Place the gourd aside with the opening up in a spot where it will not tip and spill.

7. Cut your stick or dowel to the right size for a rattle handle, usually 6–8 inches long. Check to be sure the top of the stick fits snugly into the bottom of the gourd. Shave off a little wood at a time if it is too thick. You may want to lightly sand or paint the handle as well.

8. When you are ready, lay the gourd on its side, so the seeds stay inside. Line the inside of the opening with glue, taking care not to pour glue into the space where the seeds are. Insert the stick or dowel.

9. If you plan to wrap the connection between handle and gourd with leather or other fabric, do that now.

10. Support the handle in the correct position, without spilling the seeds onto the glue, until the glue dries completely.

11. Wrap the top of the handle and the bottom of the gourd tightly with the leather or cloth strip. Then add any additional decorations you would like. Allow the glue to dry completely before using.

Rhythm Web Game

1. Have an adult or older child start. For this game, each person will need a rattle, drum, or other rhythm instrument, though clapping hands and legs work just as well. Explain that each person has his or her own special voice. Each person's voice is important, and we need all voices to make the world a good and happy place where all people and things are cared for and respected. Tell the children that their voices are probably different but when we all share our true voices, we can make beautiful things happen, such as music. Let them know that this game is about sharing our heart's voices and feeling how we are all connected in a beautiful web of energy.

2. The leader starts by playing a rhythm he or she wants to play. Then the leader passes the sound randomly to someone else in the circle. That person should then play whatever rhythm comes from the heart and then pass it on randomly to someone else in the circle.

3. Continue to randomly pass on the rhythm, creating a web of connected strands of sound.

4. When the leader feels the time is right, he or she tells everyone to join in and play together. Allow the group enough time to begin to harmonize and feel the joy in the playing.

Chapter 7

Summer Solstice

Also known as Midsummer, the longest day of the year brings light and beauty to all things. This is the Sun God's last hurrah as the light begins to wane the next day. It is a wonderful time to honor the God Within and have some fun with him.

Midsummer's Eve is believed to be sacred to the fairies. It is a special time when they are more accessible to interested humans than at many other times of the year. Visiting gardens or woods or streams may just allow you a glimpse of the Beautiful Folk.

Altars and Sacred Space

The Sun is in its prime and so we offer you a special type of altar cloth to bring the power of the Sun into your sacred space. And warm summer days are an ideal time to quiet the mind while walking a labyrinth. Then relax and chill out with some iced solar tea and yummy Sun cookies.

Sunlight Shadow Altar Cloth

As the Sun reaches its climax with the longest day of the year, the wheel of time turns once more toward darkness and we celebrate the bright energy within all of us. Make a Midsummer altar cloth imprinted with sunlight and shadow in honor of this solstice and all that you have accomplished so far this year.

Sun-activated dye is simple to use, and many of Nature's gifts will cast beautiful permanent shadows on your altar cloth. Almost any small object can be used for the decorative silhouettes in this project, but it is especially nice to capture one of Mother Nature's shapes. Oak and ivy leaves, flower petals, feathers, sprigs of herbs, or sheaves of wheat all make lovely silhouettes. Alternatively, you may wish to draw your shadow with sand sprinkled into the shape of a spiral, pentagram, or other symbol. And of course, you can always use a cutout paper silhouette.

Materials

- blank natural-fiber altar cloth
- pushpins
- orange and yellow Sun-activated dye
- 2 plastic cups
- water
- foam or sponge brushes
- shadow objects
- iron
- spray bottle
- sheet of foam board (slightly larger than altar cloth)

1. Stretch the altar cloth out smoothly onto a sheet of foam board. Then pin it in place with a few pushpins.
2. Mix each dye color by diluting 2 tablespoons of dye with 4 tablespoons of water in a plastic cup (more for a large altar cloth).
3. Spritz the altar cloth with water from a spray bottle until the entire cloth is damp.
4. Use a sponge brush to paint swirls of orange and yellow Sun-print dye all over your altar cloth.
5. Arrange your shadow objects on the freshly painted altar cloth.
6. Leave the cloth in a sunny spot free from breezes and away from little hands and paws.
7. Once the fabric is completely dry, carefully remove all of the shadow objects and unpin your altar cloth.
8. Set the dye permanently by ironing the altar cloth with a hot iron.

Walking Labyrinth

Ancient labyrinths have been found all over the world with many cultural origins and varying pathway patterns. Unlike the confusing playful maze that is built to lose and confuse us, the labyrinth is a spiraling path that may twist and turn, but it will always bring us to the center and then lead us home.

Walking labyrinths take up a lot of space, so make sure you have plenty of room. The path of a temporary labyrinth can be created using anything from piles of snow or fallen leaves to luminarias or tiki torches. A permanent labyrinth can be made from rocks, shells, wood, paving stones, flowerbeds, or shrubs. Liz made her labyrinth from the used but very sacred rocks from our sweat lodge.

Our labyrinth pattern works well for either walking or finger labyrinths. This design includes an open center space that works particularly well with a walking labyrinth because it gives you room to place a small altar and pause comfortably or gather a few people together at the center.

We recommend that you sketch out a small labyrinth on paper several times first. This will help you connect with the energy of the labyrinth and give you a greater understanding of how this design works. Your labyrinth can be made methodically with the use of a compass (or length of string) to give perfectly tidy lines or freehand for a more organic look.

Labyrinth	Diameter	Semi-Circle Diameter	Path Width
Walking	36 inches	8 feet	2 feet

These measurements can be adapted to suit your chosen labyrinth space. Keep in mind that the central semi-circle should measure 4 times the width of the path. See the illustration here as you follow these written directions.

1. Find the center of the labyrinth space and draw a semi-circle to scale. Draw 2 temporary parallel lines down from the end points of the semi-circle. The lines should measure 7 times the width of the labyrinth's path.

2. Draw 7 circular arches around the semi-circle, each beginning and ending at the temporary parallel lines and each a path-width apart. Number the end points of each circular arch from 1 to 16.

3. Join end points 1 - 3, 5 - 7, 9 - 11, and 13 - 15 together with a horseshoe loop that extends one path width from the 2 points.

4. Join end points 4 - 12 across the central path and 8 -16 down the center.

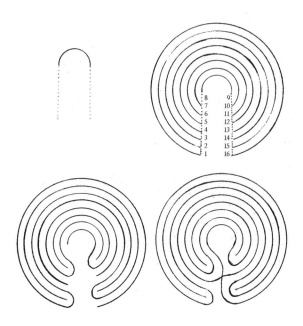

Labyrinth

Walking the Labyrinth

Walking the labyrinth is a journey for the soul, a meditation in motion. Working with the labyrinth can help give insight into questions and situations, heal illness, resolve conflict, soothe grief, or simply help you unwind from a stress-filled day.

- Take a moment to focus and establish your intent at the threshold of the labyrinth.
- Let go of your negative thoughts, release your burdens, breathe deeply, and relax.
- Walk as you feel is right at the time. Go with the flow, use your intuition, do it your way.
- Pause for a moment at the center, opening yourself to the flow of the earth and the magick of the labyrinth.
- Notice that the journey out of the labyrinth brings you back from meditation and into the moment.

Labyrinth walking can be a solitary experience or shared with friends. You may be surprised how easily kids of all ages naturally attune to and have fun with a labyrinth. Whereas Kristin's son usually walks purposefully and with great intent, Liz's little ones love to run around the twisting path. They all have fun and laugh together. Other times, we'll walk with our kids and talk together, holding hands and connecting with each other.

Tools and Oracles

At the height of the Sun God's reign, yet on the eve of the dark half of the year, we bring you two crafts symbolic of each type of energy. The staff, representing mastery and power, and tarot cards, that allow us to peer into the shadows offer a magickal balance to this section.

Staff

This is a symbol of authority, of mastership over one's spiritual tradition and, hopefully, one's own life experience. It is the *animus mundi,* or World Tree, that connects our world with other realities. The staff is often used to direct energy, much as the wand is. But more often than not, it combines the energies of Heaven and Earth, of masculine and feminine, of God and Goddess. It is a powerful experience, to craft a staff for yourself on your spiritual path. Will yours connect you with other realities or balance your personal yin and yang?

Materials

- paper and pencil
- tracing paper
- sandpaper, coarse to fine
- wood oil
- small knife or Dremel tool
- leather or colored fabric
- optional: wood-burning tool

- optional: stones, feathers, etc.
- adhesive suitable for use on both porous (wood, fabric) and non-porous (stone, metal) surfaces
- large piece of wood, head high and approximately 4–6 inches around

1. Sketch out a design for your staff. Decide what symbols you want on it and where. Consider how you want to use stones, feathers, and fabric. Plan it all out first.

2. Remove any remaining bark and sand the wood smooth. Begin with the coarse sandpaper and move up to a finely sanded surface.

3. Transfer any symbols or words onto the wood using the tracing paper.

4. Tracing the image on the wood with a knife, Dremel, or wood-burning tool, cut or burn these images into the surface. See the wood-burned footstool altar in Chapter 2 for specifics on using wood-burning tools.

5. Using a pencil, measure around any stone cabochons or crystal balls you want to attach to your staff. Using a knife or Dremel, carve out a shallow hollow for each stone. Please wear gloves to protect your hands when carving with a knife. For a crystal ball, which might look nice at the very top, hollow out a seat for the ball that is approximately ⅓ the diameter of the ball.

6. Oil the wood well at least 3 times, allowing it to dry between applications.

7. Fill the hollows with adhesive and place the stones, holding them until the glue dries enough for them to dry in place without support.

8. Place the leather or fabric where you want it. You might want to add a dab of adhesive to ensure that it stays in place, even if you are tying it on.

9. Add any remaining decorations.

Tarot Cards

Tarot is an ancient method of divining the future and allowing us to gain insight into situations that may be hidden from obvious sight. There are a huge number of tarot cards on the market. It seems there is very nearly something for everyone. But to craft your own set of tarot cards truly aligns this oracle with you, your needs, and your particular set of symbols. When you make your own, there is no need to learn meanings from a book because your deck is a part of you. It makes for a truly powerful tool.

The description that follows is for a traditional tarot deck. Keep in mind that your deck need not follow this format. Explore the traditional cards and card suits and decide what form is right for you. You may not even want to have 78 cards or any suits at all. Trust your instincts and go with what feels best.

Materials	
• at least 78 index cards	• optional: tracing paper
• scissors	• craft glue
• pens, pencils, and crayons	• textures, glitter, scrapbook papers, etc.
• old magazines and newspapers	
• paper	• peel-and-stick laminating sheets

1. Plan out your card suits and minor arcana cards. The most common common card suits are associated with the four elements: air with Wands, fire with Swords, water with Cups, and earth with Pentacles. Each suit contains a king, queen, knight, page, and ace, along with cards numbered 2 through 10. Are these the associations you would use with the four elements? If not, play with other suits to see what works best for you. Try an association web to come up with ideas.

   On a clean sheet of paper, write "water" in the center. Drawing lines outward from water, write down everything that comes to mind as you hold the image and feeling of water in your mind. Some of the secondary words may give rise to additional associations.

2. Now plan your major arcana in the same way. The traditional major arcana cards are listed on page 120.

3. Find or create the perfect images to go along with your cards. Search through magazines and newspapers, and even on the Internet to find images that really work for you. You might want to add drawn symbols or draw your own images. Specific textures and colors may resonate with your feeling for a specific card. Separate each set of images and keep it with one index card.

4. You might want to round the corners of your index cards slightly to make them more comfortable to use. Then glue or draw the images onto your cards. Be sure to leave room on each for the number and name of the card.

5. When the cards are completely dry, cut the laminating sheets to fit each card. Peel back and apply, smoothing out any air bubbles with your finger as you seal them.

6. Put them in your tarot casting bag and you are ready to divine the future!

Traditional Major Arcana Cards			
0	The Fool	11	Justice
1	The Magician	12	The Hanged Man
2	High Priestess	13	Death
3	The Empress	14	Temperance
4	The Emperor	15	Chains
5	High Priest	16	The Tower
6	The Lovers	17	The Star
7	The Chariot	18	The Moon
8	Strength	19	The Sun
9	The Hermit	20	Judgment
10	The Wheel	21	The World

Crafts

If you're going to make special tarot cards, you will need a special bag to go with them, won't you? Of course you will, and that is the first craft we present here. In the warmth of summer, we love to decorate ourselves with beautiful, but cool, clothes and body art. We offer you two of our favorite summer fun ideas for personal decoration and finish it all up with a smaller, personal version of the labyrinth. It's not big enough to walk, but following it with a finger will lull you into the same meditative state as the larger, traditional version.

Tarot Casting Bag

The best thing about making this circular bag for your tarot cards is that it opens out into a casting cloth! Make a magickal bag from cotton or velvet and line it with cotton or silk of a contrasting color or pattern. Jazz up your bag with the addition of beads and decorative ribbon. If you want to emboss a velvet bag, see Chapter 3 for directions on embossing velvet.

Materials

- string
- bag material
- pencil
- paper
- scissors
- lining material
- needle and thread
- ⅛-inch cord
- safety pin
- sewing machine (optional)

1. Measure a piece of string 3 times the length of your tarot cards.

2. Hold one end of the string stationary. While holding a pencil at the other end, draw a circle on a large piece of paper.

3. Using the paper circle as a template, cut out a circle of outer bag material and a circle of lining material.

4. Cut and sew two ½-inch buttonholes directly opposite each other 4–4 ½ inches in from the outer edge of the bag material (not the lining).

Tarot bag pattern

5. With wrong sides together, pin and loosely stitch the bag and lining together.

6. Sew a ½-inch hem around the edge, leaving a 3-inch opening.

7. Turn the bag right-side out and slipstitch the opening together.

8. Sew 2 full circles 3 and 3½ inches from the outer edge. Enclose the buttonholes within these 2 circles.

9. With the bag wide open, use your safety pin to thread the cord into one buttonhole, all the way around the bag and back through the same buttonhole. Tie the ends together. Thread the second yard of cord through the opposite buttonhole in the same manner.

10. Finish off the cord strings by fraying the ends into a tassle or adding decorative beads.

11. Pull on the cords to open and close the bag.

Henna Body Art

Mehndi (*pron.* me-HEN-dee) is the Persian name for the intricate art of painting the body with henna. This colorful tradition is a sacred art that has been used for thousands of years in magickal ceremonies around the world. Because the painted were believed to be blessed with protection, good fortune, and transformation, the Egyptians used henna to color hair and paint hands and feet in this life, and for the dead for their life in the afterworld. In India, many brides are still painted with a lacy web of paisley flowers. This ritual takes many hours and is all part of the bride's transition into womanhood.

Mehndi color will vary greatly depending on a number of factors. The most important ingredient is the henna powder, which should be finely ground with nothing added. True henna powder mixed with just water will give good color. The addition of lemon juice and the properties of some essential oils such as lavender, rosemary, and tea tree will encourage the henna mix to disperse more color and give a darker, longer-lasting color in a shorter period of time. It may help to use a brew of dark tea to mix the paste, if you want a darker color.

The potency of your mehndi mix will be at its peak when it forms a brown crust but it will lose its color strength over time. Hot weather will speed up the color release and shorten its life span. Keep your mixture fresh indefinitely by storing it in an airtight container in the freezer.

Materials

- 3 tablespoons henna powder
- 3 tablespoons lemon juice
- ceramic bowl
- dash of lavender oil
- water
- plastic wrap or foil

- fine paintbrush
- small, fine-tipped cake icing bag or plastic applicator bottle
- optional: cotton ball and lemon sugar water (½ teaspoon sugar plus 1 tablespoon lemon juice)

---

1. Mix henna powder with lemon juice in a ceramic bowl. Add a dash of 100 percent pure lavender oil.
2. Stir in a little water at a time until the mix has the consistency of sour cream.
3. Cheek for allergic reactions by applying a small dot of mix in the crease of your elbow.
4. Loosely cover the mix and wait for the top of the mix to form a brown crust (1–4 hours).
5. Practice drawing with your henna mix on a scrap piece of paper.
6. Apply the henna paste to your skin. Paint directly from the mix with a fine paintbrush or fill a small, fine-tipped cake icing bag or plastic applicator bottle with the mix.
7. Wait at least 1 hour before scraping off the paste.
8. For maximum depth of color, keep the applied pattern moist for several hours by dabbing lightly using a cotton ball and lemon sugar water.

Batik Sarong

The art of batik dates back to the sixth century and has its roots in Southeast Asia, Africa, India, and other regions. Mud or rice paste was originally used as the resist medium to prevent the penetration of fabric dyes. Most modern artists use a blend of beeswax and paraffin wax for the resist today. This is melted and drawn onto the fabric with a special batik tool called a tjanting. A tjanting is a pen-like tool with a small copper or brass bowl at the tip. The bowl acts as a reservoir, holding the hot wax as it pours through a small spout onto the material.

Sarongs provide the ideal canvas for a batik design. A batik sarong can be used as a wall hanging, tablecloth, or a throw to liven up frumpy furniture. And of course, sarongs are great fun to wear as a skirt, dress, or shawl.

Materials

- at least 8 pushpins
- charcoal pencil
- paper: copy and tracing
- candy thermometer
- paraffin wax
- beeswax
- double boiler
- tjanting
- optional: oven mitts
- optional: cookie cutter
- buckets

- fabric dye
- sarong material: thin white cotton, linen, or silk
- plastic sheet
- large pot or canning pan
- wooden spoon
- brown paper or newsprint
- iron
- wooden frame with inside measurements the same as your sarong

1. Wash the sarong in hot soapy water. Cut and hem as you wish with or without a tassel trim.

2. Plan your design and colors on regular paper. Using a black dye in combination with other lighter colors will give a dramatic effect. If you need help transferring any designs or symbols, sketch them on the tracing paper with a charcoal pencil. Then transfer that image to the sarong material.

3. Tack the top edge of your sarong to the frame at 12 o'clock with a pushpin. Stretch and pin the opposite side of the sarong on to the frame at 6 o'clock. Follow with 3 and 9 o'clock before stretching out the corners of the fabric. Add more tacks until the sarong is taut and even all around.

4. Sketch your chosen image in a paint-by-numbers style with a charcoal pencil.

5. Melt the wax in a double boiler with water in the bottom pot and the wax in the top. Place a candy thermometer in the wax and keep the temperature at 170 degrees F. Add water in the bottom pot when necessary. Never leave hot wax unattended.

    NOTE: Paraffin wax will crumble as it dries so the addition of beeswax makes a more pliable line. A balanced combination of the two waxes will crackle as it dries, allowing fine lines of dye to seep into the fabric. This crackled effect adds that unique batik look. Start with 3 parts paraffin wax to 1 part beeswax. If you prefer more crackle, add more paraffin wax. For less crackle, add more beeswax.

6. Place a sheet of plastic under the stretched sarong. Then go over the design, enclosing each color section in its own island of wax.

    Fill the tjanting's little bowl with hot wax. Hold a scrap of cloth up to the spout as you move the tjanting to the sarong. Quickly trace the charcoal outline with wax from the tip of the tjanting, refilling it as necessary. With oven mitts on, dip the rim of a cookie cutter in the wax and use it as a stamp to make a wax outline on your sarong.

    Once the outline is complete, dip a paintbrush in the hot wax to fill in any parts of your design that you wish to remain white.

7. Dip the sarong in a bucket of the lightest color of dye for the appropriate amount of time. Rinse out the excess dye with cool water and hang it out to dry. The dye bath must be kept below 95 degrees F to prevent the applied wax design from dissolving.

8. When the sarong is dry, stretch it on the frame.

9. Brush wax onto the areas that you want to remain the first color. Re-wax any areas that have crackled more than you wish. Scrunch up parts for more crackle.

10. Plunge the sarong into the second color of prepared dye. Rinse with cool water and hang to dry.

11. In a large pot or canning pan, submerge the sarong in boiling water. Stir the sarong around with a wooden spoon.

12. As the wax melts, it will float up to the top of the water. Skim off the melted wax with the spoon.

13. Take the sarong out of the water and hang to dry.

14. Sandwich your sarong between sheets of brown paper or newsprint. Then use a hot iron to melt the wax into the paper. Replace the paper

when it gets saturated with wax. Continue this process until the ironed paper is wax-free. Most handcrafted batik will have traces of wax left in the fabric. However, dry cleaning will remove these last traces of wax if you like.

Finger Labyrinth

This handheld miniature labyrinth is great for home or office. Allow yourself to escape into the sacred journey of the labyrinth as you trace its path with your fingertip. You may be surprised by how refreshed you feel after taking just a few moments to "walk" around this small spiraling path. And Kristin's husband Dave discovered that it doubles as a fun game when used with a small marble. See the labyrinth and his favorite "Zen" marble on the top of our cover.

Materials

- tracing paper and pencil
- rotary tool (Dremel) with round bit
- sandpaper (coarse and fine)
- optional: wood stain
- flat piece of wood (round or square, at least 8 inches wide)

1. Trace the outline of your wood onto a piece of tracing paper. Pencil a labyrinth to scale within that outline (create your own or use the labyrinth design presented earlier in this chapter). Draw over the lines of your sketch on the backside of the tracing paper. Transfer the labyrinth sketch by retracing the original outline on the wood.

Labyrinth	Diameter	Semi-Circle Diameter	Path Width
Finger	9 inches	2 inches	½ inch
Finger	18 centimeters	4 centimeters	1 centimeter

2. Practice carving closely aligned, curved lines on a scrap of wood with the rotary tool and round bit. When you are ready, carve the labyrinth into your piece of wood.

The pencil lines of the labyrinth represent the walls. The path of the labyrinth is the twisting spiral that swirls between those walls.

Starting at the opening of the labyrinth, carve a shallow line along the path and into the center of your labyrinth. Gradually deepen the path by repeatedly carving out a little of the path at a time.

3. Once you are happy with the carving of your labyrinth, smooth out any rough spots with coarse sandpaper. Finish off with fine sandpaper.

4. If you want to stain the wood, apply the wood stain at this point, according to the manufacturer's directions.

5. With time and continuous use, the oils from your fingers will slowly build up, adding a nice sheen to the path of your labyrinth.

Magickal Delicacies

What could be more in tune with the Summer Solstice than solar tea and Sun-shaped butter cookies? As you enjoy these delicious treats, feel the light and energy of the Sun fill your every cell, revitalizing you as it warms you and brings happiness to every bite.

Solar Tea

This is slow and easy way to make tea—just right for lazy summer days. It's also a great project for kids. Solar tea is never as hot as traditional tea, but it is ideal over ice! For a perfect summer tea, try citrus or cooling mint.

Materials

- 6 teaspoons loose tea or teabags
- tea ball for loose tea
- 2-quart clear glass container with cover
- 1½ quarts cold water
- optional: sugar or honey
- optional: lemon

1. Place tea ball or bags into the glass container. Add water and cover.

2. Set in sunlight for 2 to 3 hours. Taste to determine the strength you want. You may need to move the container every now and then to keep it in the sun. Remember that sunlight shining through glass can start a fire so keep your brewing tea away from combustible materials.

3. Remove the tea ball or bags.

4. Serve over ice with sugar or honey and lemon, if desired.

5. Store in the refrigerator for no more than 24 hours to prevent bacterial growth. If tea develops a syrupy texture, discard.

Sun Cookies

If you're going to have solar tea, then you really need some yummy Sun cookies to go along with it. These mouth-watering treats won't fail to make you smile!

Materials

- 1 cup butter
- 1 cup sugar
- 1 egg
- 2 teaspoon real vanilla extract
- 2½ cups all-purpose flour
- ¼ teaspoon salt
- 2 large bowls
- rolling pin
- electric mixer or wooden spoon
- plastic wrap or foil
- cookie sheets
- wire racks
- optional: Sun-shaped cookie cutters
- optional: small butter knife

1. In a large bowl, cream the butter and sugar until light and fluffy.
2. Add the egg and beat slightly. Stir in the vanilla.
3. In the other bowl, combine the flour and salt.
4. Add to the sugar mixture and stir.
5. Using plastic wrap or foil, cover the dough and chill for 1 hour.
6. Chill cookie sheets and preheat oven to 400° F.
7. Roll dough out onto ungreased cookie sheets. Cut into Sun shapes with cookie cutters or a knife. You might want to give your little Suns happy faces for an even more delightful treat.
8. Bake for 5 to 10 minutes until lightly golden at the edges.
9. Remove cookies from cookie sheets and allow to cool on wire racks.

Traditions From Around the World

In Romania around the Summer Solstice, women and children create a type of doll called the Caloianul. This Rainmaker doll is decorated with flowers and carried in a procession to a river or stream. At the river, the Caloianul is thrown into the water. The river is believed to carry him to the land of the rains where he then sends the rains back to the villager's fields.

In honor of the Romanian Rainmaker, we offer you a different type of magickal poppet or doll.

Chakra Healing Poppet

As is the Caloianul, poppets are magickal dolls. Used predominantly for healing, these little effigies cast a potent spell and must be treated with respect. Making a healing poppet is a wonderful way to focus loving energy, helping to heal a friend or loved one.

Materials

- a clean sheet of paper
- scissors
- needle
- 2 pieces of felt, 9" × 12"
- thread in the colors of the chakras (see the chart on page 130)

- fabric from clothing belonging to the person to be healed
- filling: healing herbs, cotton batting, healing stone(s), a lock of hair or small photo of the person
- pink or green cloth

1. Cut out a paper template in the shape of a gingerbread man.
2. Use the paper template to cut out 2 felt gingerbread men.
3. With right sides together, sew the two fabric pieces together, leaving an opening at the top.
4. Turn the poppet right side out (a pencil with an eraser tip will help reach the reach the poppet's hands and feet).
5. Fill the poppet with a combination of healing herbs (see Chapters 3 and 4), healing stones (see Chapter 8), and cotton batting. Add a lock of hair or small photo of the person to be healed.
6. Sew the opening closed.
7. Sew on the poppet's eyes, mouth, and hair.
8. Sew on spiral chakras with the corresponding color of thread. (See chart on page 130.) Start at the center of the spiral and circle the spiral outwards in a clockwise direction.
9. Make clothes for the poppet from clothes belonging to the person to be healed. This will surround the poppet with that person's energy and help strengthen the connection between poppet and person.

Colors of the Major Chakras	
Root	Red or Black
Abdomen	Orange
Solar Plexus	Yellow
Heart	Green or Pink
Throat	Blue
Third Eye	Indigo
Crown	Violet

10. Wrap the poppet in pink or green cloth as you visualize a healing bubble surrounding the person to be healed.

As you make the poppet, keep in mind that you are crafting a tool for healing. To work with your poppet, hold it in both hands and visualize your loved one as a healthy, happy person. Send this energy into the poppet. It may help to create a simple chant to help you raise that healing energy—perhaps something such as this:

Poppet of magick, I ask you to send
Healing and love eternal to my friend.

Once the poppet's work is done, give it to your friend as a gift.

Kid Stuff

Rain is a blessing in the heat of summer. Kids love to play in the rain, jump in puddles, and make mud pies. In honor of the Caloianul and the healing, life-giving summer rains, we bring you a kid-friendly way to make rainsticks. These really convey the sound of rain and are much gentler on the ears than most rattles.

Rainsticks

The rhythm of running water is one of the most healing of sounds, and many cultures have developed musical instruments that simulate these soothing sounds. The native people of Chile have used ceremonial rainsticks for hundreds of years. Shamans summon gods in the hope that the rain spirits will bless the land with life giving rain. The rainstick is a wonderful magickal tool whose sound conjures up powerful images of cascading rain, even in the most barren of deserts.

The traditional South American rainstick uses the skeleton branches of the quisco or capodo cactus. The dead hollow cactus is then punctured with the sharp spines from a live cactus. Small volcanic pebbles tumble over the internal spiral of cactus spines creating a rain-like sound. It takes about 70 years to grow a cactus rainstick. Making your rainstick from recycled materials is less demanding on the slow-growing cacti and more kind to the environment.

Materials

- cardboard mailing tube with end caps
- newspaper or junk mail
- small kitchen sponge
- white emulsion paint
- acrylic paints
- paintbrush
- Plexiglass
- tape

- hammer
- 1 pound of nails the same length as the mailing tube (use more nails for longer tubes)
- tumbling ingredients: dry rice, dry beans, beads, or very small stones
- papier-mâché paste: 1 cup of craft glue mixed with 1 cup of wallpaper paste

1. Hammer the nails in an evenly spaced spiral just below the spiral groove that runs down the length of the mailing tube.

2. Hammer the remaining nails in a spiral just below the first spiral of nails.

3. Close one end of the tube with an end piece. Pour the tumbling ingredients in the open end.

4. Close the open end and test the sound of your rainstick by slowly turning it upside down. Add or subtract the tumbling ingredients until you are happy with the sound.

5. Tear old newspapers or junk mail into 1-inch strips.

6. Mix a batch of papier-mâché paste.

7. Saturate the strips of the paper with the paste, then stick them onto the rain stick.

8. Use a small kitchen sponge to smooth out an even layer of glued paper strips over the rainstick.

9. Glue on 2 or 3 more layers of paper strips and allow the rainstick to dry overnight.

10. When the rainstick is completely dry, paint with a primary coat of white emulsion paint.

11. When the primary coat is dry, paint images of sky and rain with acrylic paints.

12. To make an extra fancy rainstick, replace the end caps with circles of Plexiglass cut to size. Keep the see-through ends in place with a little tape and a rim of papier-mâché. Watch the stones cascade over the internal spiral of nails through the peepholes at each end of your rainstick.

Chapter 8

Lughnasadh

Hot summer days, cool drinks made from harvested grains, frozen deserts, and good friends. That's what this time of year brings to those of us in the northern hemisphere. Named for the Celtic hero, this is a feast day honoring him and his foster mother, Tailltiu, who died clearing the forest of Brega. In her memory, Lugh created the Telltown Games to be held every year on the anniversary of her death.

This first of the harvest festivals is still a time of merriment, fairs, and games. We gather together in the warmth of summer to give thanks for the harvest and strengthen the bonds of community, delighting in homemade foods, sharing stories, and having fun. This is a time of joy, reflection, and friendship.

Altars and Sacred Space

The plants around us have given us a season of beauty and grace. And as they move into the beginning of their harvest season, so do we. We work with plant energies and reflect upon our own harvests. However, at this time of year, we may be vulnerable to the energies we have reaped over the course of the year. So at Lughnasadh, we offer you a protective shrine and a blessing from the plant world.

Shelf Altar

This little altar/shrine is a mix inspired by the Chinese altars of Thailand and the beautiful Spanish tinwork of New Mexico. Traditional Chinese altars are painted red for protection. In the same way that a Buddhist shrine does, these little altars form part of the daily ritual where water, food, incense, and flowers are offered to the Buddha, gods, and ancestors.

New Mexican tinwork flourished along the Santa Fe Trail in the mid-1800s when Spanish colonists started recycling the discarded tin cans that had been used for oil and food by the American army. The scrap metal was transformed into candlesticks, mirror frames, and crosses that were ornately engraved with indented lines and nail-punched holes. On the bottom right side of our cover, you can see one version of this glowing red and gold shelf altar.

Materials

- 1 inch by 8 inch pine plank, 20 inches long
- ¾-inch dowel (at least 18 inches long)
- red acrylic paint
- thin tin sheet (silver, brass or copper)
- carpet tacks or brass escutcheon pins
- hammer
- 6 drywall screws
- dry ballpoint pen
- drill with ⅛-inch, ¼-inch, and ¾-inch drill bits
- saw
- scissors
- ruler or tape measure
- optional: nail for hanging on a wall

1. Cut the plank into one 10-inch-long and two 5-inch-long pieces.

2. Cut the dowel into two 9-inch pieces.

3. Drill two ¼-inch deep holes with a ¾-inch drill bit centered exactly ¾ inch from each edge of two corners of both of the smaller (5-inch) panels along a 7-inch top edge.

4. Paint the 3 wood pieces and the 2 dowels with an even coat of red acrylic paint.

5. If you wish to hang this shrine on a wall, measure across the back of the rear panel and find the center point 1 inch down from the top. Drill a small upward-slanting hole ¼ inch deep with a ¼-inch drill bit.

6. Cut a piece of tin 5 inches by 7 inches. Then use scissors to scallop the edge.

7. Pressing firmly with a dried-out ballpoint pen, impress your design into the back of the tin. Pierce the holes with a tack and hammer if desired.

8. Nail the border of the tooled tin to the center of the 10-inch panel with escutcheon pins or carpet tacks.

9. Push the dowel rods into the pre-drilled holes, connecting the top and bottom pieces.

10. Line up the back section with the back of the top and bottom pieces. Drill 3 evenly spaced holes through the back panel, directly into the top and bottom sections with the ⅛-inch drill bit.

11. Assemble your altar by drilling the dry wall screws into the 6 pre-drilled holes.

12. Add decorative edging with scalloped strips of tin to the top and bottom sections of your altar with carpet tacks or escutcheon pins.

13. If you wish, use a nail to hang it on your wall.

Smudge Sticks

At Lughnasadh, the energies of the plants are very much on our minds. We harvest grains for bread and beer, fruit and vegetables for our tables, and many of us begin to harvest sacred herbs for smudge sticks and incense mixtures. The creation of your own smudge sticks is a simple yet sacred craft that provides you with wonderful gifts to give and means of purifying your sacred space all year long.

Though sagebrush and cedar are the most common smudge stick plants, you may want to personalize yours. Kristin's son adds rosemary and lavender to his smudge sticks, along with either pine or sagebrush. (See the list of magickal herbs in Chapter 4 for suggestions.)

Materials

- sacred plants 7–12 inches long
- scissors
- paper bags (1 for each plant)
- a bottle of water or other offering
- cotton thread
- newspapers or a towel

1. Take your scissors, water, and paper bag(s) out on a plant walk, in your yard or in a wilderness area. Do not pick near a road.

2. Before picking, take a few deep breaths and ask to meet the eldest plant in the area. Trust your instincts and make an offering of water to that plant. Ask permission to harvest some of the local plants for sacred use.

3. Harvest only what you need or feel is appropriate from each plant. Place your cuttings into the paper bag. When you are finished, give thanks to the plants and the place.

4. Allow the plants to dry before wrapping into sticks. In some areas, mold can grow if they are wrapped too soon or if they are stored in plastic containers. You may hang them or leave them in the paper bags to dry.

5. When the plants are dry, gather together enough to tightly fill the space between your index finger and thumb, if you touch the tips of both fingers together to form a circle. Some people prefer thicker smudge sticks, so add as much as you like for the stick you want.

6. Beginning where you cut the stems, tightly wrap the bottom of the stick and knot it. Wrap it again at least 3 times and knot the string once more.

7. Spiraling up the stick, continue to tightly wrap the plants. Wrap the bunch 3 times at the top, 1 inch before the tip of the bunch. Knot your string and spiral back down to the bottom. Knot the string again and cut off any excess.

Tools and Oracles

In a community, it is important each voice be heard and that we listen to spirit guidance as we create our vision for local and global communities. To that end, we offer you a talking stick so that in your gatherings each person may speak without interruption and be heard with respect. And vision incense may be just the thing to help you gain insight into yourself, various situations, and the community at large so that you might be properly prepared to speak and create.

Talking Stick

The talking stick is a profound Native American traditional tool that has as much to do with listening as it does with talking. A talking stick can be made by you as an individual or by the group of people for whom the talking stick is intended. The talking stick is used when you have something important to say or share with others. It is equally important to listen—not just hear the words, but also truly listen with your heart and soul to what the speaker is sharing with you.

Materials

- stick or dowel, 8–10 inches long
- sandpaper
- leather or fabric
- wood-burning tool or paint
- glue
- string or leather cord
- optional decorations: feathers, fur, crystals, charms, or beads

1. If you have chosen a natural stick, decide whether or not you want to leave the bark on. If you prefer a smoother stick, remove the bark and sand it smooth.

2. Using a wood-burning tool or paint, decorate the stick with words or magickal symbols. These should be aligned with the intent for your talking stick. You may want to use it to resolve conflict within your family, to encourage honest and open communication, or to share wisdom and grow spiritually as a group.

3. Add any additional decorations you want. You might consider having each member of your group contribute a bead or charm that can be strung onto to the talking stick. As members leave or join, you can always adapt the string.

4. Dedicate your stick to your chosen intent and begin to create your magick.

5. When working with a talking stick, find a comfortable space where you will not be disturbed. Sit in a circle. Working in a clockwise direction, take turns holding the stick and speaking. Hold the stick with both hands ether held horizontally in front of you, connecting your energy with that of the group, or vertically with one end of the stick grounded on the Earth. The first person to speak should establish the intent and focus of the talking circle.

Vision Incense

To create magick requires vision. The truth is that we create each and every day. We can choose to do this consciously and create joy or we can do it unconsciously and see what happens. If you would like a little boost to your visioning, try meditating while burning this wonderful incense.

Or if your group is willing, burn a bit of this during meetings to encourage wisdom to flow through each of you. And if you just aren't ready for an involved incense-making procedure, simply grind the herbs in a food grinder or mortar and pestle, place about ½ teaspoon of your mixture on a charcoal disk, and light.

Materials

- 1 teaspoon gum tragacanth or gum arabic
- glass or bowl of warm water
- wire whisk
- wet cloth
- 1 part mugwort (*Artemisia vulgaris*)
- 1 part cinnamon
- 1 part sage (*Salvia officinalis*)
- saltpeter (potassium nitrate)
- 6 parts powdered sandalwood or cedarwood

- 2 parts powdered benzoin
- 1 part ground orris root
- 6–9 drops essential oil (myrrh or sandalwood)
- waxed paper
- small kitchen scale
- ceramic or stoneware bowl
- food grinder
- thin wooden skewers
- Styrofoam square to hold skewers

1. To make tragacanth gum glue, which you will need later in this project, dissolve 1 teaspoon of ground gum tragacanth in a glass or bowl of warm water. You may need a wire whisk to help it all dissolve. Believe it or not, gum tragacanth can absorb a gallon of water in a week. Just let it soak up the water until it reaches a paste-like consistency.

    If you plan to make stick incense (more difficult than cones or blocks), thin it out with more water. You don't want it too thin, but it should not be dough-like the way you need it for blocks or cones. A little practice will show you just the right consistency. Don't worry about the bitter smell; it won't affect your incense.

    When you have the consistency you want, cover with a wet cloth and set aside for later. If it gets too thick while sitting, just add a little more water and mix well. Whatever you don't use will keep for a month.

2. Prepare your incense mixture. Grind together 1 part each of mugwort, cinnamon, and sage to form a powder.

3. In a bowl, mix the wood, benzoin, and orris root well.

4. Add essential oils and mix well.

5. Add 4–5 parts incense mixture to the oil mixture.

6. Weigh and add 10 percent saltpeter. Do **not** add more than 10 percent. Mix well.

7. Add tragacanth gum glue and mix well. Form into blocks or cones on waxed paper.

   For stick incense, dip the skewers into the mixture. Stick them, incense-side up, into the Styrofoam and allow to dry slightly. Dip 4–5 times until they are as thick as you want them. Then stick them back in the Styrofoam and allow them to dry completely.

8. Allow to dry for 2 to 7 days in a warm place until thoroughly dry.

Crafts

Our crafts for this season are perfect for summer's end. We bring you a Green Man tree spirit to represent the living Earth and the life-giving harvest, t-shirts to enjoy the last of the warm days, a solid but glittering arch to hold a statue or candle, and a special necklace to connect you with the elements as you move into the dark half of the year.

Tree Spirit

Whether walking through woodland or forest, it is easy to feel the life force radiating from the trees and plants around you. It's no wonder so many of us are quite literally tree huggers. This Green Man image is a tribute to the spirit in every tree and represents the vital energy of the living Earth. At this time of Lughnasadh, you may want to create a true Green Man, such as the one on our cover, to remember him in his prime as we move into the dark half of the year. Or you may prefer to adapt the colors to represent the harvest and coming autumn.

Materials

- large pin or needle
- rolling pin
- oven
- baking tray

- 26 gauge wire, 6–8 inches long
- 2-ounce packs of polymer clay in the following colors: chocolate brown, sand, pearl, black, green, and leaf green

1. Mix one pack of chocolate brown clay with one pack of sand-colored clay. Knead them together until the clay is pliable and the two colors swirl together like marble.

2. Form half of the marbled brown clay mix into a flat 4-inch-wide circle.

3. Shape a nose from some of the remaining marbled clay and mold it onto the center of the circle.

4. Roll out 2 pearl-colored balls each about the size of a marble.

5. Roll out 2 green-colored balls each about the size of a pea.

6. Roll out 2 black-colored balls each about ½ the size of a pea.

7. Stack the green balls on the pearl balls. Then stack the black balls on the green. Firmly press these 2 stacks onto the 4-inch circle to make the eyes.

8. Shape the teeth by rolling out a small sausage of pearl clay. Then flatten it a little before carving lines with the point of a pin to separate the individual teeth. Press the teeth into place on the 4-inch circle.

9. Use the remaining marbled clay to form the chin, lips, cheeks, eyelids, and brow.

10. Marble-mix the 2 green colors together as you did the browns.

11. Roll out the marbled green into a 1/8-inch-thick slab with a rolling pin.

12. Use the pin or needle to cut out 10–12 leaf shapes from the green slab.

13. Arrange the leaves around the face to form the Green Man's hair and beard. Then attach each leaf by pressing some part of it firmly in to the face.

14. Push a small hoop of wire into the back of the face at a central, top position. This hoop will be used for hanging.

15. Bake in the oven according to the manufacturer's directions.

16. Hang on a wall, above your altar, or in your favorite tree and enjoy.

Mosaic Candle Arch

Shimmering shards of light radiate in all directions from the flame of a single candle under the eave of this beautiful mosaic arch. See the candle arch on the left side of our cover for an idea of how it might look when you are finished. Add a panel of colored glass to the back of the arch to make a delightful window shrine to house a statue of your favorite deity.

Materials

- aluminum flashing
- shoebox
- duct tape
- 1 inch by 6 inch plank of wood
- a flat wooden board
- screws and screwdriver
- ready-mix cement
- chicken wire
- saw
- sand or stones
- water-resistant, cement-based tile mortar
- small broken pieces of mirror or mirror tiles
- small spatula or palette knife
- damp lint free cloth
- optional: acrylic paint
- small colored glass mosaic pieces or small mosaic tiles
- optional: large piece of colored glass, glass cutter, metal ruler, metal file

1. Wrap a length of aluminum flashing around the outer side walls of an empty shoebox to make the inside arch. Take care to keep the bottom of the box and the edge of the flashing perfectly in line.

   NOTE: Always wear gloves when working with aluminum flashing. The edges can cut the same way a knife can.

   Bend an arch shape around 1 narrow end of the box.

   Shape the 2 bottom corners of the arch by folding the flashing and then opening out the fold to fit the corner angle.

   Overlap and tape down the ends of the flashing to the box with duct tape. Keep the arch shape by taping the flashing to the bottom and top of the box at the 3 straight sides.

2. Cut out a rectangular-shaped piece of wood board that measures 4 inches longer and 4 inches wider than the finished shoebox arch.

3. Cut the 1 inch by 6 inch plank to make a frame that fits around the top edge of the board. Screw the 4 corners together to finish the frame.

4. Screw the wood frame to the top of the board with several screws pushed in from the back of the board in to the bottom of the frame.

5. Give the frame an arch shape by bending a piece of aluminum flashing inside the frame. Curl the flashing around 1 short end and against the 2 long sides inside the frame. Tape the ends against the side of the frame.

6. Position the small arch inside the large arch. Then weigh down the small arch with sand or stones inside the shoebox.

7. Line up the edges of the arches symmetrically to form the arch-shaped moat that will form the mold of your arch.

8. Sprinkle a layer of sand over the floor of the mold to prevent the cement seeping under the arches. Mix up about 35 pounds of ready-mix cement according to manufacturer's directions.

    NOTE: Always wear a dust mask and eye protection when mixing cement.

9. Lay a 2-inch-wide strip of chicken wire around the moat to help strengthen the form.

10. Slowly and evenly, poor the cement into the moat, completely covering the chicken wire. Take care to distribute the cement all around the form without shifting the small arch. Leave the cement arch to dry completely.

11. Disassemble the wooden frame then push out the smaller arch frame.

To Mosaic the Arch

1. Prepare the water-resistant cement-based tile mortar according to the manufacturer's directions.

2. Use a small spatula or palette knife to spread a thin layer of mortar over 1 small area at a time. The depth of mortar will depend on the thickness of mosaic piece being used. You want the mosaic pieces to sit firmly in place with the mortar about halfway up the thin side of each mosaic piece.

3. Firmly press each mosaic pieces into place with a little space between them. Working from the bottom up, mosaic the inside of the arch with mirror pieces. Mosaic the front, back, and sides of the arch with small, colored mosaic pieces.

4. Wipe off all excess mortar with a clean damp cloth and leave to dry.

5. To make the grout, mix enough of the water-resistant, cement-based tile mortar to cover the whole arch. If you want to color the grout, use white mortar and add a little acrylic paint with the mix.

6. Use a spatula to spread the grout mix all over the mosaic surface of the arch. Push the grout into every little crack and crevice between the mosaic pieces.

7. Wipe the top surface of the mosaic clean with a damp lint-free cloth.

To make your arch into a window shrine, cut out an arch-shaped piece of colored glass 1 inch larger than the inside arch. Fix the glass to the back of the arch with the mortar before you mosaic the rest of the arch.

Wear eye protection and gloves when cutting glass. Using a metal ruler as a guide, hold the glass cutter perpendicular to the glass and press down firmly as you make one single stroke to score a straight line on the smooth side of the glass. Snap the glass along the score line by breaking the glass along the strait flat edge of the metal ruler. Unless you are experienced with cutting glass, cut the curved top of the arch with several straight lines (more like an octagon than a circle). Sharp or rough edges can be smoothed with a metal file.

Elemental Necklace

This beautiful necklace is simple to make with representatives of all four elements: air, fire, water, and earth. Spirit is what you bring to this beautiful piece as you charge it with your own energy. Kristin made bright pink and blue ones for each of our kids, but three of our other favorites can be found on the cover in the top right. Use a clear crystal or choose a magickal stone from the list on page 144 for a truly personal creation.

Materials

- 1 crystal or other stone, 3–4 inches long
- leather or suede in your favorite color
- craft knife
- leather or suede cord in a complementary color
- craft glue
- small shell, approx. 1–2 inches long
- 2 small feathers
- glass pony beads

1. Cut a leather or suede rectangle, approximately 2 inches wide and 4 inches long.

2. Wrap the top ¼ of the crystal in the leather to be sure the size is right. At least 1 inch of the crystal needs to be covered, and you need at least 1½ inches of extra material above the crystal.

3. When you have the size right, glue the material to the crystal and allow to dry overnight.

4. Cut a ½ inch by ½ inch hole in the top part of the material, above the crystal.

5. Angle or round the material above the cut. Trim off any excess glue on the surface of the crystal.

Magickal Stones

Amber	purification and protection, patience
Amethyst	catalyst for change, connection to spirit guidance and personal intuition
Aquamarine	protection, meditation, calming influence
Azurite	connection to spirit guidance, creativity, relaxation
Chrysocolla	emotional healing, reconnection with Nature, self-esteem and self-love
Citrine	protection, energetic balance, stability, manifestation, clarification
Clear Quartz	magnifies energy, connection to spirit guidance and personal intuition
Hematite	grounding, protection, concentration, balancing, cooling and calming
Jade	dreaming, harmony, access to spirit guidance, emotional strength
Jasper	protection, energy balancing and stabilizing
Lapis Lazuli	intuition, psychic awareness, creativity, dreaming, protection
Malachite	transforming, emotional clarity and healing, balancing, protection
Moonstone	reflective, introspective, calming, nurturing, sustaining
Obsidian	grounding, reconnection with Nature, protection, aids with focus
Rose Quartz	heart healing, unconditional love, gentleness, calming
Smoky Quartz	grounding, dissolves negativity, protection, stabilizing
Tiger's Eye	mental clarity, access to memory, grounding, balancing
Tourmaline	clearing, energizing, transforming, balancing, protection, self-confidence
Turquoise	protection, inspiration, strengthening, grounding, aids in communication

6. Tie the cord in a tight knot around the leather top, about ¼ of the distance between the hole and the crystal. You might want to first draw a thin line of glue where the cord will lie to hold it in place. Leave 1 inch of cord hanging below the crystal.

7. Glue the shell into place just over the knot.

8. String one pony bead on each side of cord.

9. Place a drop of glue on the outside edge of each side and attach one feather to each side. Slide the pony bead down over the top of the feather and allow it to dry in place.

10. Measure a cord around your neck and to the proper length for your necklace plus 3–4 inches. String it through the hole in the leather above the crystal and knot the cord at the top.

11. Allow all glue to dry completely before wearing.

Over time, the feathers may wear down or break. If this happens, simply pull the pony beads up and remove the feathers. This may take a bit of twisting and care but you will be able to break through the glue. Simply reattach new feathers as in Step 9, and your necklace will be as good as new.

Screen Printed T-Shirt

Screen-printing allows you to print a single design multiple times. So you can make several shirts or print your design on a t-shirt and then make a matching tote bag or banner. The possibilities are limitless! Check out the labyrinth tote bag that Liz made on the left side of our cover. Now we all have labyrinth t-shirts too! So why not whip up a batch for friends and family and head out for one last outdoor gathering before the cold winds of winter arrive?

Materials

• paper and pencil	• 4 coins
• 9-inch squeegee	• fine-tipped paintbrush
• drawing fluid	• 3 teaspoon measures
• a few sheets of clean flat paper	• duct tape
• screen filler	• sheet of plastic
• screen printing fabric inks	• 10 inch by 14 inch wooden screen printing frame
• soft lead pencil	

1. Sketch out your chosen design on a sheet of paper.

2. With the mesh-side down, frame-side up, line the inside edge of the wooden frame with duct tape, extending the tape ¼ inch onto the mesh and creating a waterproof ledge around the mesh.

3. Place your design under the screen and trace the image onto the mesh screen with a soft lead pencil.

4. Elevate the frame, mesh-side down, by placing a coin at each corner. Protect your work surface with a sheet of plastic.

5. Use a fine-tipped paintbrush to paint your design with the drawing fluid, then leave it to dry completely.

6. Keep the painted frame elevated with the coins. Spoon 3 teaspoons of screen filler onto the duct tape ledge at 1 narrow end of the screen.

7. Use the plastic squeegee to spread a smooth even coat of screen filler over the mesh screen, making no more than 2 swipes with the squeegee. Then leave it to dry.

8. Put a few sheets of clean flat paper inside the t-shirt to act as a paint barrier and padding. Lay the t-shirt on the prepared work surface. Then smooth the t-shirt out so there are no folds in the fabric.

9. Position the frame directly on top of the t-shirt so that the image is exactly where you want it to be on the shirt.

10. Spoon 2 teaspoons of fabric ink halfway along 1 duct-taped ledge. Then spoon 2 more teaspoons of fabric ink of a contrasting color along the second half of the same ledge.

11. Hold the screen down firmly with one hand as you spread the paint smoothly across the screen with the squeegee in the other hand. Keep the squeegee at a 45-degree angle, pressing the paint through the mesh onto the fabric as you push the squeegee back and forth across the screen a few times.

12. Lift the screen from the t-shirt. Lay it out to dry while you print out more t-shirts, tote bags, or other objects.

13. Wash the screen thoroughly with warm soapy water any time the prints become blurred or the paint starts to dry out on the screen, or when you have finished printing. Once the screen is dry it will be ready for printing again.

Magickal Delicacies

The bounty of the land is evident in these delicious treats, perfect for a warm day at the beach, a picnic lunch at your favorite park, or a celebratory outdoor ritual. Sit back, relax, and enjoy this harvest season in true style!

Mead

Mead is a truly ancient beverage that was enjoyed by peoples around the world. In fact, some say it is the oldest fermented beverage. Who are we to argue with such an ancient and widespread tradition? It is an ideal beverage for any Lughnasadh celebration, but to craft true mead requires training and experience. So we offer you this delicious quick mead as a modern alternative. As you drink, raise a glass to the delectable lineage of mead, from the Norse and Celts to the Greek and Assyrians. To your health, wealth, and joy!

Materials

- 6–8 ounces honey, preferably local
- 1 gallon white wine
- 6–7 citrus or spice tea bags
- large stockpot
- glass bottles or jars

1. Mix honey, wine, tea bags, and fruit in a large stockpot.
2. Bring to a boil for 1 minute, then simmer 2–3 minutes.
3. Let cool, then transfer to glass bottles or jars and refrigerate for 3 days.

Melon Sorbet

Melons are cooling and wet in the heat of the summer Sun. Enjoying a watermelon or cantaloupe straight out of its rind is wonderful at any time. But for festival occasions, we prefer a melon sorbet. For an extra special touch, serve it using the half rind as a bowl.

Materials

- 4 cups melon, cut into small pieces
- ½ cup granulated or superfine sugar
- 1 tablespoon lemon juice
- optional: 1 tablespoon dark or spiced rum
- blender or food processor
- coarse sieve
- wire whisk

1. Puree the melon in a blender or food processor and strain through a coarse sieve.

2. Combine ½ cup of pureed melon with the sugar and bring to a boil, stirring frequently.

3. Remove from heat and add to the remaining pureed melon. Add the lemon juice and whisk well.

4. Cover tightly and freeze overnight. If you choose to add rum, do it just as the sorbet begins to harden in the freezer.

5. Spoon into bowls or refrigerated melon rinds. Garnish with berries and top with honeyed whipped cream.

Honeyed Whipped Cream

As if fresh whipped cream wasn't delicious enough, this topping is a dessert in itself. Serve it on melon sorbet or warm muffins, or simply dip fresh fruit into it. Yummmm!

Materials

- 2 ounces cream cheese
- ½ cup whipped heavy cream
- 2 tablespoons honey
- wire whisk

1. Whisk the cheese and honey together until smooth.

2. Fold in the whipped cream.

Traditions From Around the World

Raksha Bandhan is a Hindu festival focusing on the wearing of sacred threads for protection and to remind the people of their connections to the ancestors, Rishis, and the Vedas. In northern India, the raksha is tied by sisters around the wrists of their brothers, offering them protection in the year to come. In other areas, the holy threads are given to open the way for wisdom and as a gift from spiritual patrons. Sometimes the raksha hold amulets of love and protection. Whether one gives or receives the raksha, it forms a bond of love between them, reminding us all of the beauty of both giving and receiving freely in relationships.

Friendship Bracelet

In honor of the beautiful Raksha Bandhan and the sacred threads, we offer you the friendship bracelet. May this craft strengthen your connections and deepen your love.

┌─ Materials ─┐

- beads of various colors and sizes
- air-drying clay
- paint or pencil

- large pin or skewer slightly thicker than the rope
- 3 lengths of natural fiber rope, twice the length around your friend's wrist

1. Decide on a symbol that will represent your relationship with the person you are making this bracelet for. You may want a heart for love or a yin/yang for the wonderful balance of your friendship. Choose something that will be meaningful for both of you.

2. Craft a small bead from the clay. Using the pin or skewer, poke a hole through the bead and ensure that it is large enough for the rope to fit through.

3. If you want to carve your design onto the bead, do that now with the pencil and allow it to air dry according to the manufacturer's directions. If you prefer to paint your design, wait until the clay is dry, then allow the paint to dry before proceeding.

4. Begin by knotting all 3 lengths of rope together, leaving a few inches of rope free to tie the bracelet onto your friend's wrist. Then braid the rope, adding beads as you wish by looping a length of rope through the holes.

5. Using your wrist to estimate length, place the bead you made at the center of the bracelet. Then finish the bracelet in the same manner. Knot all 3 lengths at the end, leaving a few inches of rope free to tie the bracelet onto your friend's wrist.

6. Tie the bracelet onto your friend's wrist. If you wish, you may want to follow the lead of Raksha Bandhan and chant a mantra as you knot the ropes, such as this:

> *Protection and love, I tie into this knot secure.*
> *May our friendship be blessed forever more*
> *And may love and trust always endure.*

Kid Stuff

Harvest time is the perfect time to remember that great web of life and how we all depend on each other. Kids innately recognize that all creatures are enlivened by a Divine spirit. They see it the first time they gaze with wonder on a cricket, a baby duck, or a kitten. Art is just one way that we can encourage those natural understandings and help them create more peaceful, loving futures for themselves and all people.

Bird Feeders

Baby birds have fledged and are stuffing themselves to prepare for the big migration. Building special bird feeders with your kids is a wonderful project to teach them about bird biology and ecology as well as how to honor the connections all things share. Place this near a window so you can all sit unseen, watching the birds as they come and go. And offer a prayer that they might live through the dark times to return to your feeder with their young next year.

Very young children can do this simple alternative feeder largely on their own: Cut a star or circle out of heavy cardboard (or use a pinecone), smear it with peanut butter, and sprinkle it all over with bird seed.

Materials

- 7-inch light plastic plate
- twine
- hot melt glue gun
- ¼-inch wooden dowel, 6 inches long
- drill with ½-inch and ¼-inch bits
- ¾-inch paper fasteners
- duct tape
- acrylic paint
- small knife
- bird seed
- plastic tube with end caps

1. Paint the plastic tube and allow it to dry completely.

2. Drill two ½-inch holes all the way through the feeder: one 2 inches above the bottom of the tube and the other 3–4 inches above the bottom.

3. With the small knife, cut 2 small slits in the top cap, parallel to each other. These will hold the twine for hanging.

4. Cut one ¾-inch slit in the bottom cap and in the center of the plastic plate.

5. Glue the plastic plate to the bottom cap or bottom of the plastic bottle, lining up the slits and inserting 1 paper fastener through both to hold them in place.

6. Fold open the metal tabs on the inside of the bottom cap. Duct tape them securely down and allow the glue to dry.

7. Glue the bottom cap to the plastic tube.

8. Insert the dowel through the lower hole. Duct tape in place from below the holes, if necessary.

9. String the twine through the holes in the top cap to a length that will allow the bird feeder to hang in view and be accessible for refilling. Duct tape over the holes.

10. Fill it with bird seed and duct tape or screw the top cap onto the tube.

11. Hang the bird feeder by a window and get ready to watch your feathered friends.

Chapter 9

Autumn Equinox

K nown by some as Mabon or Alban Elfed, this is the official start of the fall season. Scarlet, gold, and orange leaves light up the trees and in some areas even the grasses glow with deep reds, blues, and purples. Days are still warm but evenings may bring us a taste of the chilly winds to come and we start to think of soft blankets, warm drinks, and the fresh tastes of the apple and grape harvest. The changing of the light and the cooler weather spurs many wild creatures to begin their long migration.

At this time of year, we begin to prepare for winter on many levels. Not only are we breaking out the sweaters and scarves, but our spiritual energies are also turning inward. Divination and personal shadow work are popular at this time of year, along with magick of protection and prosperity.

Altars and Sacred Space

As our minds move away from the external, outdoors type of ritual, we offer you two wonderful projects for a more inward, indoors form of ceremony. Although both may be used outdoors as well, these are truly unique ways to work in harmony with the dark half of the year.

Cross-Stitch Altar Cloth

Embroidery is used to weave words and images onto fabric. When each stitch is made with magickal intent you are truly weaving a spell into the fabric of the world. The equal-armed cross has many symbolic meanings. The four points of this little cross remind us of the four seasons, the four directions, and the four elements. In the junction of two paths we may perceive the crossing over from life to death, from night to day, from one world to the next, and from the physical to the spiritual. The cross is also an ancient symbol of protection.

Cross-stitch is a simple little stitch that can transform a small piece of woven cloth into a beautiful image well worth framing or a plain tablecloth into a treasured heirloom. The cross-stitch pattern is usually an uncomplicated design, and the background fabric usually remains unstitched. With a little imagination, you will be able to create a beautifully embroidered altar cloth that will last for many years. The repetitive action of cross-stitching can be quite relaxing and meditative, just right for a journey into autumn and winter.

Materials

- cross-stitch fabric or aida cloth
- cotton or silk embroidery thread
- #24 or #26 cross-stitch needle
- scissors
- graph paper
- colored pencils

1. Plan out your cross-stitch design on graph paper, using colored pencils to represent each color of thread you will use. Use 1 square of the graph paper to represent a single cross-stitch.

2. Separate the cross-stitch thread by first cutting a 10-inch to 20-inch length of thread. Fan out the 6 threads at 1 end. Pinch the tip of 2 threads together and gently pull them away from the remaining threads. Divide the 4 threads into 2 groups of 2 and use them when needed.

3. Beginning at the most central point of the design, and using your graph paper template as your guide, cross-stitch outward from the center until you have a completed design.

4. A cross-stitch is made in the shape of an "X." Each X is made from 2 diagonal stitches that cross at a central point. Make a stitch by bringing the threaded needle up through the hole at the bottom left-hand corner of a square and down through the hole at top right-hand corner of the

same square. Finish the stitch by bringing the needle up through the bottom right-hand corner of the same square and down through the top left-hand corner of the same square.

Work as many stitches as you can from a single length of thread in each area, but do not stretch the thread to get to a square more than 5 squares away from the previous stitch. Rather than knotting the loose ends of thread, run the last few inches of thread under 4 or 5 of the stitches on the backside of your cross-stitch design.

Portable Stone Circle

We know a few people who have installed incredible miniature Stonehenges in their yards. These are wonderful places to do moving meditation or ritual. But not everyone has the time, space, and money to do that. And some of us need to be able to dismantle the circle when we are not using it for various reasons. What's more, this allows you to bring the energies of an outdoor ceremony inside for autumn and winter rituals. This is a stone circle that anyone can create, even in a very small space. It is fully portable and you need not spend a fortune on it, unless you choose to.

Materials

- 4 large anchor stones: yellow, red, blue, and green

- tape

- pencil or small wooden stake

- compass

- 12 smaller stones: 2 yellow, 1 orange, 2 red, 1 purple, 2 blue, 1 blue-green, 2 green, and 1 yellow-green

- a string that measures half the distance across your desired circle

1. Tape the end of the string to your pencil or stake. Stick this firmly into the ground in the center of where you want your circle. If you are creating an indoor circle, simply place a stone on the end to hold the string in place.

2. Using your compass to determine the directions, extend the string to the east. Place the yellow anchor stone there, in the place of the rising Sun, the element of air, and new beginnings.

3. Extend the string to the south. Place the red anchor stone there, in the place of the transformative element of fire and passion.

4. Extend the string to the west. Place the blue anchor stone there, in the place of the element of water and emotion.

5. Extend the string to the north. Place the green anchor stone there, in the place of the fertile Earth and grounding strength.

6. Remove the string and arrange the other stones into equidistant positions between these larger stones. For example, moving south from the east anchor stone, you will lay one yellow stone, then one orange stone, then one red stone before you come to the red anchor stone.

7. If you are creating a larger circle, add more stones as necessary. You may prefer to use color variations that gradually go from yellow to red, for example.

Tools and Oracles

Though no one can be certain just how this festival acquired the name Mabon, we do know that the Mabon is the child of light, son of the Great Mother, who was taken from her soon after his birth. He was recovered by Arthur and his companions on a brave quest, as told in the Welsh myth of Culwch and Olwen. In honor of the Mabon and this wonderful ancient tale, we present the leather scabbard. And because our magick turns to divination at this time of year, we bring you the simple yet powerful pendulum. May both bring you the greatest of blessings.

Leather Scabbard

Whether you work with a small athame or a long-bladed sword, there is something sensual about sliding your blade snugly inside a perfectly fitted, beautifully embossed leather scabbard. This magickal union simply belongs together. Not only will the scabbard protect your blade, it will also allow you to wear your sword comfortably.

Leather is sold by the ounce per square foot. Heavy leather is thicker and more durable than lightweight leather. A small athame sheath can be made with a 4-ounce weight of leather; a large heavy sword will need the 6- to 10-ounce weight of leather. Keep in mind that heavy leather can be quite a challenge to work with.

Materials

- your sword
- thin cardboard
- pencil
- leather or utility knife
- awl
- multi-pronged hole punch
- rubber mallet
- waxed thread
- needle

- blade-sized sheet of paper
- liquid leather dye
- leather wax cream
- dye solvent
- soft, lint-free cloth
- stitch groover
- sponge
- brush for leather dye
- modeling tools: stylus-point and spoon- and ball-shaped

1. Make a scabbard template by laying your sword flat on a sheet of thin cardboard and tracing around the outline of the blade. Follow the exact line at the top of the blade where the hilt meets the blade.

2. Draw a ½-inch border around the blade outline (¾-inch for a thick blade). If your blade has a waistline, do not tailor into this narrow contour. You will not be able to slide the fatter tip of the blade through the thin waist of the scabbard.

3. Cut around the outer border to make the scabbard template.

4. Trace 2 template outlines onto the smooth side of the leather with the point of an awl. If your blade is not symmetrical you must turn the template over before cutting the back section of your scabbard.

5. Follow the awl's indented line with a leather or utility knife and carefully cut out the scabbard pieces.

6. To make a belt loop, cut 2 parallel lines in the back scabbard piece. These slit lines should run vertically together starting at least 1 inch down from the top edge. Cut these parallel slits about 1 inch apart. The length of the slits should be about 1 inch longer than the width of your belt.

   Set the stitch groover to ¼ inch and carve a narrow groove around the sides and tip of both scabbard pieces on the smooth side.

7. Punch out the stitching holes by holding the punch vertically in place and striking the punch hard with a rubber mallet.

   NOTE: The stitching holes must be perfectly in line when the front and back sections are sandwiched together, so take great care to line up the first holes precisely. Keep each hole within the channel of the carved groove and use a multi-pronged hole punch to help keep the stitch holes inline. If you only have a single-hole punch, run the wheel of a stitch marker tool around the carved grove to mark out even-spaced stitching holes.

8. Use your awl to pierce through tough-to-punch holes.

9. Stitch the front and back sections together with waxed thread and needle using a double running stitch. Tie off the thread with a double knot.

10. If you want to add a design on the surface of the scabbard, sketch out that design on a blade sized sheet of paper with pencil. Practice Steps 11 and 12 on a scrap of leather before working on your scabbard.

11. Use a moist sponge to dampen the leather lightly and evenly. Trace the outline of your design onto the front of the scabbard with the rounded point of a stylus-point modeling tool. Once you have finished tracing the outline, remove the pattern and finish impressing the image by rubbing various spoon or ball shaped modeling tools on the leather to further impress the design.

12. Brush a little liquid leather dye on a scrap of leather. If the color is too strong, dilute the dye with a little dye solvent. Brush a light film of the dye over your finished leather scabbard.

13. Buff the dry scabbard with a soft, lint-free cloth.

14. Finish off with a good coat of leather wax cream. Once the cream is dry, polish the leather surface with a soft, lint-free cloth.

Pendulum

Perhaps one of the simplest of divination tools, the pendulum is powerful and accurate enough to be used by people from all walks of life. Even many healers use the pendulum for diagnosis and divination. Although a very simple pendulum can be made by simply looping a string through one of your favorite rings, and you can always purchase one of the pricey weighted pendulums, a beautiful personal tool can be crafted by your own hands with ease.

Materials

- crystal point
- paper and pencil
- soft aluminum craft sheets, 36-gauge
- gold jewelry wire, 26-gauge
- glass or metal adhesive
- scissors
- silver or gold necklace chain
- toothpick
- thick sewing needle
- optional small stone cabochon

1. Cut out a paper rectangle long enough to wrap all the way around the crystal and wide enough for ½ the width to cover ¼ to ⅓ of the top of the crystal. The ends can either meet in the back of the crystal or slightly overlap. Experiment to be sure you have the size and shape correct before using this template to cut out your metal piece. Although aluminum can be smoothed out after use, small crease lines will remain and the finished pendulum will not have a clean, smooth metal surface, so it is best to practice with the paper first.

2. Trace around the paper template onto the aluminum and cut out the metal rectangle.

3. With a toothpick, smooth a small amount of the adhesive onto one side of the metal.

4. Wrap the metal around the top part of the crystal, taking care to keep the bottom line even all the way around. As you go, press gently and the metal will mold itself to the shape of the crystal. Allow the adhesive to dry.

5. Above your crystal will be a small aluminum tube. With the front of the crystal facing you, use your thumbnail to gently crease each side of this tube in toward the center. Taking the front and back between your index finger and thumb, press these sides together, folding the crease inward so you now have 2 flat surfaces (1 in front and 1 in back). Use your nail or the handle of your scissors to further flatten and smooth these surfaces.

6. Using the sewing needle, poke a hole in the center of this flat surface, all the way through the back. This is where the chain will go through, so you may need to poke a few holes in a circle and push out the center to make the opening large enough.

7. If you want to add a stone cabochon to the front of the metal, decide exactly where to place it. Dab on some adhesive and place the stone. Allow the adhesive to dry.

8. With a toothpick, smear a line of adhesive on the back of the aluminum casing. Beginning right at the edge of the aluminum on the back, begin to spiral the gold wire up the top, over the adhesive line, ending in the back just below the opening for the chain. Allow the adhesive to dry.

9. String through your chain and you are ready to go.

Crafts

All of our Autumn Equinox crafts involve the blessings of the land and the fruits of the harvest, including the sore muscles that may result from too much hard work. Delight in the cornucopia, pray with a special bowl, keep the beauty of the leaves throughout the winter, and soak away tension in a soothing bath.

Beaded Prayer Bowl

The art of the Mexican Huichol Indians has a powerful symbolic language that is used to express deeply held spiritual beliefs. Beaded gourd bowls known as jicaras are made as prayer offerings (niekira). The gods and goddesses drink from the jicaras and absorb the essence of the prayer "written" in the beads. Huichol shamans communicate with the spirits through niekira in ritual to ensure a good harvest, bring healing and balance, send prayers, and give thanks.

We went with a Celtic version of the jicara, as you can see in the bottom left corner of the cover. Use whatever symbols or images speak to you and your spirit allies, and you are sure to craft a work of beauty and magick!

Materials

- clean, dry, hard-shell gourd
- paper and crayons or colored pencils
- utility knife or small hobby saw
- pencil
- sandpaper
- metal spoon
- water
- clean tin can
- small pot
- beeswax or beadwax
- wide paintbrush pin
- seed beads in various contrasting colors

1. Create a color sketch of your prayer design to scale before proceeding.

2. Select a gourd with an even, round shape that sits stationary on its base. To make a bowl from the bottom half of your gourd, pencil the bowl rim around the gourd just below the widest part of the gourd.

   NOTE: Work outside and wear a dust mask and rubber gloves when cutting and cleaning gourds.

3. Following the penciled rim line, slowly and carefully cut through the gourd skin with a utility knife or small hobby saw, holding the gourd steady as you cut.

4. Scrape the seeds and pulp out of the bowl with the edge of a metal spoon.

5. Smooth the rough edges of the rim with sandpaper.

6. Put the wax in a clean tin can. Put the can in a pot. Add water to the pot, halfway up the outside of the tin can and gently heat the water. Keep an eye on the wax as it melts. Once all the wax has melted, turn off the heat.

   Working on a warm day or in a warm spot in your home will help keep the wax soft and easy to work with. Remember to keep your finished beaded bowl away from direct sunlight or excess heat as the wax may melt and destroy your beautiful prayer.

7. Brush a few even layers of melted wax around the inside of your gourd bowl.

8. Lightly scratch the basic outline of your design in to the brushed wax.

9. Start beading in the center of the bowl. Using the scratched outline and a color sketch of your design as a guide, pick up one bead at a time with a pin and place it where you want it, push each bead about ¾ its width into the wax. Focus on your wish or prayer as you work.

10. Keep your beaded prayer bowl in a special place that is sacred to you.

Cornucopia Basket

Throughout history the cornucopia has been used in art and literature to represent fruitful abundance and fertility. According to one Greek myth, the goddess Rhea bore five children. Her husband Cronos swallowed each child and kept them in his belly so that they would not be able to overthrow him and take his place as the king of gods. When Rhea bore a sixth child (Zeus), she hid him on the island of Crete, where he was raised by nymphs. The gentle goat Amalthea nursed baby Zeus with her milk. When the young Zeus accidentally broke off one of Amalthea's horns, he filled her broken horn with a bountiful supply of fruits and flowers. Later Zeus placed Amalthea with her horn of plenty among the stars.

Baskets are sometimes used to hold offerings of food for the gods. Other baskets have spiritual images woven into them. The cornucopia is similar to the magick cauldron of the Celtic Dagda with its never-ending supply of fulfillment. Both cauldron and cornucopia are symbolic of the fulfillment of life and dreams as much as the fulfillment of the belly. Make your own cornucopia basket in the autumn or spring from the long, supple trimmings of vines or choose your weaving material from a basketry store.

Materials

- 14–20 vines, at least 24 inches long
- string
- big tub of water
- vine bark, fine vine or colored thread
- acorn or small crystal
- harvest vegetables, fruit, or autumn leaves

1. Separate the vines. Trim any adjoining vine branches or leaves, but keep each length of vine as long as possible.
2. Wind each length of vine into a coil and tie with string.
3. Soak your vines in a big tub of water overnight.
4. Sort the vines by length and width. Take 7 short thick vines and cut them 24 inches long.
5. Bunch the 7 vines together and bind them tightly at 1 end with a long strand of vine bark, fine vine, or colored thread.
6. Push an acorn or small crystal into the center of the tied vines to help open out the long spokes of the bundle and add a little extra magick.
7. The spokes will widen with each loop of vine to make the horn shape of the cornucopia but you can control the curve and width of your basket by the tightness of your weaving.

   Starting with a long, thin flexible vine, tuck 1 end into the center of the bundle. Working in a clockwise direction, weave the vine outside the bundle, over one spoke under the next, then back out and over the following spoke. Continue to weave under and over and so on in a continuous spiral. This type of weaving is known as "randing."

8. Once you have finished winding a vine, tuck its end inside the basket and under the previous loop of vine. Tuck the end of a slightly thicker vine under the top loop of vine and continue weaving in and out of the spokes.

9. Add more vines and continue weaving until you have woven halfway up the length of the 7 spokes.

10. Bend the remaining length of each spoke around the back of its left-hand neighbor and then outside the horn. Thread the end of each spoke through the its neighboring top loop. Finish off the rim by neatly tucking and trimming the end of each spoke.

11. Fill your cornucopia basket with harvest vegetables, fruit, flowers, or colorful autumn leaves.

Paraffin Leaves

Deciduous trees offer a gorgeous contrast with the evergreens, as their leaves explode in a glorious riot of colors. This is Nature's main event of autumn! They are so beautiful and so ripe with the energy of the season that we love to bring them inside to decorate our homes and altars.

Materials

- paraffin wax
- colored leaves
- tongs or tweezers
- wax paper
- pencil or other tool for inscribing in wax

1. Melt the paraffin according to the manufacturer's directions.

2. Using the tongs or tweezers, quickly dip your leaves into the melted paraffin and set aside on wax paper to dry.

3. Once they are dry, gently inscribe them with your name or special words and symbols.

Bath Salts

A chill wind blows outside and a warm, soothing bath awaits you inside. What better way to end a long hard day (or any day) than with a healing soak in the tub? Light some candles, lower the lights, and day-dream yourself into a beautiful land of fantasy. This wonderful recipe makes about 3 cups of bath salts, enough for 6–12 baths.

Materials	
• large mixing bowl	• ¼ teaspoon glycerin
• 2 cups Epsom salts	• 6–7 drops essential oils
• 1 cup Kosher salt	• clean glass jars

NOTE: See the magickal plants table in Chapter 4 for oil ideas.

1. Mix the Epsom and Kosher salts together in the large bowl.
2. Add the glycerin and essential oils and blend well.
3. Fill the jars and close tightly. Use ¼ to ½ cup in your bath.

Magickal Delicacies

The fruit harvest is full of apples, grapes, and berries, as well as the first of the dried foods that have been prepared for winter. Picture a bright fire burning in a mosaic firepit, the flames glinting off the mirrored tiles. Friends and family share laughter as they pass around fun popcorn balls and hot drinks. It doesn't get much better than that!

Hot Mulled Wine

Let's see: changing leaves, grape harvest, cooler temperatures—it must be time for hot mulled wine! You would be hard pressed to find a more delicious autumn treat.

Materials	
• non-aluminum pot	• peel of 1 lemon
• 1 bottle of red wine	• peel of ½ orange
• ⅔ cups sugar	• paring knife
• ½ cup water or brandy	• wooden spoon
• 7 cloves	
• 1 teaspoon nutmeg	• ladle
• 2 cinnamon sticks	• 2 mugs

1. First choose your wine. This is not the recipe to use either the cheapest or the most expensive wine for. Try a deep, full red in the middle price range.

2. Pour the wine into the pot over low heat. Be sure the wine does not boil during this process.

3. Add remaining ingredients except cinnamon sticks and allow it to heat slowly until hot to the touch, stirring occasionally.

4. Ladle the wine into the mugs, leaving the seasonings behind. Garnish each with a cinnamon stick and serve hot.

Popcorn Balls

Popcorn balls are not just for kids! They are a perfect addition to a mug of hot mulled wine or spiced apple cider. Experiment by adding a few drops of food color or mixing in some raisins or chocolate chips. This recipe makes about 12 balls.

Materials

- 9 cups popped corn
- 1 cup sugar
- 2 tablespoons butter
- 2 cups corn syrup
- optional: food coloring

- medium pot
- mixing bowl
- mixing spoon
- optional: 3–4 cups raisins or chocolate chips
- wax paper or plastic wrap

1. Boil sugar, 1 tablespoon of the butter, and corn syrup until thick. If you are going to add food coloring, add a few drops before moving on to the next step.

2. Pour mixture over popped corn and blend well. If you want to include raisins or chocolate chips, add them now.

3. Coat your hands in the remaining butter and form the mix into balls.

4. To store, wrap in wax paper or plastic wrap.

Traditions From Around the World

Higan-e, or "Ceremony to Reach Enlightenment," is a Buddhist celebration that has been honored on the Spring and Autumn Equinoxes in Japan since ancient times. The higan is the place of enlightenment. At this time of equal night and day, the Buddha is believed to return to Earth for one week to lead stray souls to Nirvana. The six days before and after the Equinox itself symbolize the Buddhist Six Perfections that are needed before we can leave the world of suffering and attain nirvana. It is believed that Buddhist practice is particularly powerful on these days.

Lotus Blossom Light

These little paper lotus lights are a charming tribute to this most magnificent lily. Lotus blossoms are flowers of great spiritual significance and can be found in many creation myths. Because the flower opens at dawn and closes at dusk, the light of the Sun is closely linked with the lotus. The Buddhist Tara sits on a lotus blossom and even the Buddha himself is often pictured sitting or rising from a lotus blossom.

Lotus light

Materials

- clean, empty tuna can
- chisel or nail
- galvanized wire (104 inches)
- needle-nose pliers
- tissue paper
- craft glue
- scissors
- soft paintbrush
- pink and green watercolor paints
- tea light
- yellow marbles or glass chips

1. Pierce 8 evenly spaced holes around the top edge of the tuna can with a chisel or nail.

2. Cut 8 lengths of 13-inch galvanized wire and fold each wire in half.

3. Thread one end of a wire into a hole in the can. Curl ½ inch of the wire over the top edge of the can with needle-nose pliers to make a small loop. Squeeze the loop tightly in place with the pliers.

4. Thread the opposite end of the wire through a neighboring hole and attach it to the can in the same manner.

5. Repeat Steps 3 and 4 with each wire until all 8 wire "petals" are attached. Note that neighboring petals share attachment holes.

6. Form each petal into the same shape.

7. Cut 32 pieces of tissue paper to the same shape as the petals with a ¼-inch border.

8. Attach 1 piece of tissue paper at a time to each wire petal by wrapping the border around the wire frame and gluing the tissue paper together. Repeat 4 times with each petal.

9. Glue crumpled strips of tissue paper strips around the outer edge of the can.

10. Gently paint the petals with diluted pink watercolor paint. Start at the tip of the petal and brush toward the center leaving the color more intense at the tips.

11. Paint the outer edge of the can green.

12. Allow to dry completely. Then refine the position of the petals.

13. Place a tea light in the center of the can. Fill the remaining space with yellow marbles or glass chips.

NOTE: To make an extra fancy version of this lotus light, add an extra row of 8 petals. First punch 16 holes. Attach the top 8 wire petals through every other hole. Then add the bottom row of petals using the remaining holes. Add tissue paper and finish as instructed here. Bend the top row of petals up and the bottom row down.

Kid Stuff

Kids appreciate the power of prayer, too. It makes sense to them, particularly the very young, that if we speak our prayers, or better yet send them out through the elements, that the gods will certainly hear and answer them. This little bit of magick can be a powerful tool in the hands of a child.

Wishing Boats

Wishing boats, made of natural materials and floated out with their candles on the strength of wind and water, really bring those concepts home to kids of all ages. They are wonderful tools to demonstrate the idea that the light remains, even during the time of greatest darkness.

Materials

- votive or birthday candle
- crayons or paint and brushes
- matches
- knife or Dremel tool
- 2 small twigs or dowels, 6 inches long

- optional: duct tape
- glue gun
- square of cotton fabric, 4" × 4"
- flat wide piece of wood, approx. 8" × 10"

---

1. Cut a small hollow into the piece of wood to fit the twig or dowel, approximately 3 inches from the front and directly in the center.

2. Cut another small hollow into the piece of wood to fit the candle, approximately 3 inches from the rear and directly in the center.

3. Write your prayers on the top surface of the wood, including any symbols or images that help your kids believe in and visualize them.

4. Glue one dowel or twig to the other, about 2 ½ inches from the top of the first dowel and directly in the center of the other, forming a cross.

5. Glue the fabric to the dowels, making a sail.

6. Glue the sail structure to the hollow made to hold the dowel or twig. You can use duct tape to give it added support if necessary.

7. Glue the candle in place.

8. Take your wishing boat to a special lake or river. Light the candle as you hold the prayer in your mind, and send it off across the water.

Chapter 10

Lunar Celebrations

T he changing shape of the Moon is a constant reminder of the cyclical nature of things and the mystery inherent in the natural world. People all over the planet plan celebrations, prayer vigils, drumming circles, and other magickal operations around the phases of the Moon. With its pull on the tides of our Earth, the power of the Moon over our bodies and our emotions is apparent. And emotion, the desire to create what you will, is a vital component in magick.

The Full Moon is generally believed to last for three days before the exact point of fullness and three days after. This is the height of the Moon's energy. Things often come to a head during this phase, and emotions may be running high. Most energy is directed outward, and people like to get together for drumming circles and prayer vigils on the Full Moon. Even so, this energy may be used for whatever you want most.

During the Waning Moon, the Moon appears to shrink. This is the time to work toward lessening or eliminating things, such as stress, weight, and unhealthy habits.

On the dark of the Moon, Her face is hidden from us, yet the power is no less tangible. Many people find that the Dark Moon increases their psychic abilities and they use this time for divination and visioning, much as we do the dark half of the year.

On the New Moon, we see the beautiful crescent in the sky. This is the time of new beginnings. Use this time to work on anything you wish to create, new things you want to bring into your life, and new patterns or abilities you want to develop.

After this, the Moon waxes toward full again. This phase is best used for an increase of something: opportunities, job offers, money, inspiration, friends, passion, and so forth.

Altars and Sacred Space

Rounded and shimmering like moonlight on the ocean, abalone shells are a perfect natural bowl. Too shallow to really use for liquids, we chose to use them to hold smudge for purification. They bring in a feminine, soothing quality to the burning herbs and the wafting smoke.

Smudge Holder

So by now, you have made your own smudge stick and fan and have performed the smudge ceremony. You definitely need something special to hold that smudge. A simple yet beautiful smudge holder can be seen in the top left of our cover. This beautiful holder is built to last and not burn through the shell to the table or your hand. By using magickal stones (see Chapter 8) in its creation, you only add to the sanctity of the space you create when you smudge.

Materials

- abalone shell
- 3 medium-sized stones
- craft glue
- small stones or fetishes/symbols
- fine gravel, sand, or crushed stone
- sandpaper
- at least 4 small stones or beads to fit in the holes of the shell

1. The idea is to create a shell cauldron, so choose 3 medium-sized stones to serve as feet for your abalone shell. They should be relatively flat on one side, to fit snugly against the shell with glue. It is also best if they have thicker ends to support the outer edges of the shell and thinner ends that will go into the center of the shell.

2. Turn the shell upside down and glue these 3 stones to the bottom. Test the position to be sure the shell sits the way you want it to. Then leave it upside down for at least 2 hours to dry.

3. Turn the shell right-side up and check the position. If it needs to be adjusted, pull off the stones, lightly sand the remaining glue off, and re-glue into the correct position.

4. Choose small beads or stones to fill any holes in the bottom of the shell. Place an excess of glue into the holes, filling them completely. Add the stone or bead and position so the hole is covered.

5. Pick a few additional stones or small fetishes/symbols to decorate the flat rim on the top side of the shell and glue these on.

6. Allow the glue to dry overnight. Cover the bottom of the shell with fine gravel, sand, or crushed stone to prevent it from cracking under the heat of a lit smudge stick or burning herbs.

Tools and Oracles

More people probably participate in drumming circles on Moon phases, particularly Full Moons, than at any single time around the year. These are times of prayer, healing, connecting with community, and just plain fun. And so we bring you the frame, or shaman's, drum.

Frame Drum

There is nothing so special as playing a drum you crafted yourself. It holds your own energy and merges that in a beautiful way with the energy of the drum itself. To offer prayers or healing through this type of rhyth-

mic partner is an unparalleled experience of joy and connection.

You might think that drum making is a difficult and involved business. It certainly can be, but anyone can craft a relatively simple drum for his or her own use. Kristin's son made his first

Drum & lacing

drum with her help when he was just 6 years old—and he dyed it forest green, even the wood! Two years later, he made his very own without any assistance. He's helped make frame drums, log drums, and all sorts of drums made from wild and crazy materials. If he can do it, so can you!

Materials

- drum round or frame
- drum skin, 6–8 inches larger than the frame
- bucket or bathtub of warm water
- towel
- ruler or long straight edge
- craft knife
- scissors
- thick pile of newspapers
- optional: carpet tacks and hammer
- pliers
- tracing paper
- optional: rope or belt
- optional: fabric dye
- colored pens or pencils
- #2 lead pencil
- high quality rubber eraser
- optional: acrylic paints, permanent markers, rubber stamps, stencils
- rawhide lace, 1½ feet per inch diameter of the frame
- optional: suede strips, ½ inch to 1 inch wide and 7–10 inches long

1. Soak the drum skin and rawhide lace overnight in warm water. If you want to dye the drum, add the fabric dye to the soaking water, according to the manufacturer's directions.

2. Remove the skin and lace. Use a towel to eliminate excess water.

3. Put a thick layer of newspaper down under the skin to protect your table. Using a craft knife, cut a slit ⅛- to ¼-inch long, just large enough to fit the lace through, at 12 o'clock on the skin. Make another slit at 6 o'clock, then at 3 and 9 o'clock. Make 2 more equally spaced slits between each of these 4. Be sure to make all cuts parallel to the edge of the skin or they may pull through when you string the lacing.

4. Place the frame exactly in the center of the skin. String the lace through 1 hole and knot it. String the long end through the opposite hole and knot it. You may choose to cut the lace here and repeat this process for the remaining holes or continue lacing around with 1 continuous lace. (Refer to the photo on page 171 to see how this should look if you cut the lace after connecting 2 holes.)

   Do not pull too tightly on the lacing. As the rawhide and skin dries, it will naturally tighten up and hold its shape.

It is helpful but not essential to knot the lace at each hole. As you lace the skin, fold the skin between holes to maintain a level edge and to keep the drumhead flat and smooth.

5. If you want a very symmetrical, smooth drum, use the carpet tacks to hold the folds in along the inside edge of the frame and tie a rope or secure a belt around the outer edge of the frame. For a more natural, freeform shape, simply let it dry as is.

6. Allow the drum to dry completely before playing. This may take 1–3 days, depending on your climate.

7. Wrap the suede around where you plan to hold the drum for a softer handle. Tie it into place.

8. Plan a full-color design for the front of your drum on a piece of tracing paper. When you have it just the way you want it, transfer the image to the face of your drum. Number 2 lead pencils will erase from the skin easily if you make a mistake. Transfers from tracing paper do not generally work well, so stencils or rubber stamps are recommended. Using permanent markers or acrylic paints, fill in the colors and allow to dry completely.

Crafts

Guess what the common theme of the crafts in this section is? How did you know? It's the Moon! Well, there may be no big surprise there but our only natural satellite possesses such mystery, power, and beauty that it deserves to have special items crafted to remind us of its light. These beautiful items add a stunning touch to any Moon celebration and they make great gifts.

Hanging Crystal Moon

The beauty of the Moon is so overwhelming, it is no surprise that people have been worshiping Moon gods and goddesses for centuries. Moon legends, monuments, and ornaments can be found all over the world. With this crystal Moon, you can honor

Crystal Moon

the Moon throughout Her phases. If you're lucky, you can catch some bright moonlight in the glass and crystals of this hanging Moon. But even during the day, direct sunlight on this little crescent Moon will cast tiny rainbow moonbeams across the room.

Materials

- needle-nose pliers
- 20-gauge silver wire
- 100 small (4 millimeter) faceted glass beads
- 1 crystal, approximately 1 inch long
- nylon thread or fishing wire

1. Use needle-nose pliers to wind a small loop at one end of a 33-inch length of 20-gauge silver wire. Refer to the photo for guidance as you follow these directions.

2. Starting at the looped end of the wire, bend the wire into a 3-inch-wide circle. Keep the circle in shape by twisting the wire around the neck of the loop.

3. Extend the long end of the wire down the center of the circle with a curve, forming the outline of the crescent Moon within the circle.

4. Spiral the remaining length of wire all around the outer edge of the Moon and then up the central crescent curve, tying the very end off in a loop, close to the first loop.

5. Tie 1 end of a 25-inch length of wire to the top point of the crescent Moon.

6. Thread 1 bead onto the wire, close to the point of attachment. Then wind the wire around the edge of the crescent shape and add 1 or 2 more beads.

7. Continue adding rows of beads and weaving the wire around the crescent in a zigzag fashion until the crescent shape is completely interwoven with beads.

8. Tie off the end of the wire at the base of the crescent.

9. Hang the crystal from 1 of the small loops with nylon thread, so that it dangles within the circle of the Moon.

10. Hang the Moon from a long length of nylon thread tied from the second loop. Adjust the little loops slightly, until the Moon and crystal look and hang just right.

11. Hang your crystal Moon in a sunny (or moonlit) window and enjoy the shining prisms of light.

Triple Moon Candleholder

This glass mosaic is the perfect addition to any lunar celebration. Made of shining silvery blue and deep rose, the light of the triple Moon shines forth in definitely goddess-like colors, giving an aura of love, light, and mystery to your celebration.

Triple Moon candleholder

Materials

- round glass bowl, approx. 3 inches tall by 4 inches wide
- glass and metal adhesive
- optional: glass star shapes
- vinyl or latex gloves
- newspapers
- toothpick
- popsicle stick
- charcoal grout
- bowl of water
- lint-free cloth
- sponge
- scrap paper
- non-permanent marker
- votive candle or tea light
- matches or lighter
- circle templates: 1⅜ inch and 1¼ inch diameters
- broken pieces of glass, pale blue and deep rose, ranging in size from approx. ¼ to ½ inch

1. Clean the glass bowl in soapy water and allow to dry completely.

2. Using the circle templates, plan the triple Moon design on a piece of scrap paper. Then transfer it with non-permanent marker to opposite sides of the glass bowl, halfway from top to bottom. If you need to adjust the design, simply wipe off the marker and start over.

3. Fit several pieces of pale blue glass into the template on the scrap paper. Completely fill the circles and crescents with glass.

4. Fill one crescent on the glass bowl with metal and glass adhesive, using a toothpick to apply the adhesive and wearing gloves to protect your hands. Apply the blue pieces of glass exactly as you have them on the paper template. Only apply 1 or 2 pieces at a time because the glue may take some time to dry. On a curved bowl, your pieces will be slipping all over the place if you do not allow them to dry into place with support.

5. Repeat Step 4 with the other crescents and circles. Allow them to dry completely.

6. Fill in the remaining space on the bowl with the rose glass pieces and optional star shapes. Leave approximately 1/8 inch between the rose pieces, stars, and the completely filled-in Moon shapes. Allow to dry completely.

7. Mix the grout with water according to the manufacturer's directions. It should be a thick paste when ready.

8. Wearing gloves, use a popsicle stick or your finger to push the grout into all the spaces between the glass. Do not cover the Moon shapes with grout. Don't worry if you get some grout on the other glass pieces.

9. Using a damp sponge, smooth the grout and remove any excess. Allow to dry for 30 minutes to 1 hour.

10. Using a damp lint-free cloth, clean any grout off all the pieces of glass. Allow to dry completely.

11. When you are ready to celebrate or meditate with the Moon, simply place a candle in the bowl and light.

Magickal Delicacies

These magickal treats will liven up any lunar celebration. Each brings in the energies and shapes of the Moon in her changing phases—and they are delicious too!

Crescent Cookies

Ancient Phoenicians once baked saffron-flavored crescent cookies in honor of Ashtoreth, goddess of fertility, fruitfulness, and the Moon. Saffron, which can be rather expensive, is optional in this recipe honoring the magickal goddesses of the Moon throughout the world.

Materials

- 1 egg
- ¾ cup milk
- ⅓ cup vegetable oil
- ¼ cup honey
- 2 cups all-purpose flour
- 3 teaspoons baking powder
- ½ teaspoon salt
- optional: ¼ teaspoon saffron
- greased cookie sheet

---

1. Mix egg, milk, oil, and honey in a large bowl.
2. Add remaining ingredients and stir until just mixed.
3. Cut into wedges and roll up, starting at the rounded edge.
4. Place on greased cookie sheet with points from the rolling down and shape into crescents.
5. Bake for 20 minutes at 400 degrees F.

Coconut Rum

Did you know that coconuts and papayas are magickally associated with the Moon? Perhaps it is due to their beautiful round shapes and pleasing tastes. Whatever the reason, this wonderful beverage will add fun and refreshing liquid to any lunar celebration.

Materials

- 2 whole coconuts
- sharp, strong knife or drill with 1-inch bit
- non-aluminum bowl
- 1 cup papaya juice
- 1–2 shots of dark spiced rum
- optional: 1 cup orange or mango juice
- ice
- blender
- fun straws
- optional: paper cocktail umbrellas

---

1. Cut a 1-inch hole in the shell of each coconut. Pour out the milk into a bowl.
2. In a blender, combine the coconut milk, juice, and ice. Blend well.
3. Add the rum and stir.
4. Pour back into the coconut shells and serve with fun straws and paper cocktail umbrellas, if you wish.

Chapter 11

Other Holidays

Once you get in the habit of creating joy throughout your life, you find that a whole host of holidays exists, just waiting to be celebrated. We bring you some of the more common and some of our favorites in this chapter. But don't stop here. Allow the energy of creation and celebration to flow through your life. Celebrate Cinco de Mayo, Buddha's Birthday, the beginning or end of Daylight Savings Time, Black History Month, or perhaps just Tuesday.

Pregnancy

In spite of feeling tired, feeling that you're as big as a house, and dealing with cravings or morning sickness, pregnancy is perhaps the most magickal time of a woman's life. To grow the body for an incoming spirit is a great blessing. It is a time full of wonder and anticipation. As such, it should be fully experienced and honored in special ways.

Tummy Cast

A truly unique method of honoring this special time in a woman's life and memorializing the look and feel of carrying your child within you, the tummy cast can be great fun. This is a rather intimate experience so it is probably best to do with your partner or closest friends. It can also get a bit messy, but the result is a very tangible monument to the fullness of your body and the promise of your child-to-be.

Magickal Crafts

- petroleum or vegetable jelly
- plastic wrap
- scissors
- rolls of pre-plastered strips
- towels
- bowl of warm water
- paper and pencil
- newspapers
- optional: sandpaper, gesso
- optional: shellac or acrylic coating
- optional decorations: crayons, markers, acrylic paint, glue, plastic flowers, photos, etc.

1. Decide just what parts of your body you want to cast. Many moms do just the belly but there are plenty that choose to include their breasts and/or upper thighs in the cast. Sitting or standing will show your fullness much better than lying down, particularly if you want your breasts cast. Be sure you will be comfortable in the position you choose for 20 to 30 minutes.

2. Lay towels or newspapers down below where you will be posed and cover any furniture you will be resting or sitting on.

3. Get the pre-plastered strips, scissors, and bowl of warm water ready to go. Cut the strips into sections ranging from 6 to 14 inches long.

4. Liberally cover the area to be cast with petroleum or vegetable jelly. Cover any areas with significant hair with a layer of plastic wrap over the jelly for added protection. Plaster that attaches to hair hurts when removed!

5. Dip 1 strip at a time into the warm water and smooth it onto the area to be cast, rolling off excess water with your fingers as you remove them from the water. Apply 3–4 layers of strips over the entire area.

6. In about 15–20 minutes, the drying plaster will begin to pull away from your skin as you move. Let it dry for at least 5 minutes after finishing the final layer before removing. When you are ready, wiggle and twist your way out of the cast. It should come off fairly easily if the plaster is dry enough.

7. Allow the cast to dry for 48 hours before decorating.

8. Choose what, if any, designs you want to decorate your tummy cast. Some women fill it with magickal symbols and family names. Others draw happy designs such as flowers and balloons. Still others wait

until the baby is born and create a collage of photos and birth announcements. Decide on what is most meaningful to you and plan it out on a piece of paper.

9. If you desire a smooth surface, sand the exterior of the cast and apply a light layer of gesso.

10. Decorate as you wish and apply shellac or acrylic coating to preserve and protect your tummy cast.

Blessing Way Necklace

A traditional Navajo healing ceremony, the Blessing Way has been adapted as an alternative baby shower for spiritual moms in recent years. This is a much less commercial and much more personal, intimate way to honor the blessed event of a birth. During Blessing Way celebrations for moms-to-be, the expectant mother is really pampered by her loved ones. They may brush her hair or give her a foot massage. Poems are read and promises of aid during delivery and after the baby is born are voiced. Candles are lit and symbolic gifts are presented. It is a truly beautiful ritual that touches the heart and soul of all involved.

Materials

- natural fiber string
- beads and charms brought to the Blessing Way celebration by loved ones

1. Gather together in a circle, with the expectant mom made very comfortable in her place. Light candles and put on soothing music.

2. Pass the string around the circle clockwise. As each person receives the string, she (or he) adds a bead to the growing necklace, sharing a story of her relationship with the expectant mom and why she chose the bead she did. She may also choose to send energetic blessings into the bead at this time.

3. When the circle is complete and everyone has added their beads, knot the string to a comfortable length for the expectant mom and place it around her neck.

4. She may choose to wear this during labor and delivery for added strength and blessings or she may keep it as a keepsake holding only the energy of this circle as a lifelong reminder of the love you all share.

NOTE: Alternatively, have each person bring 2 beads and string a bracelet for the baby at the same time.

Baby Blessings

There is no celebration quite as full of hope, joy, and love as when a new baby comes home for the first time. This most precious little one has an entire life of possibility to look forward to—and friends and family hope to all be around to see what he or she creates with this gift of physical life. We all want this beloved child to have the best. We want to provide strength and love, guidance and spiritual connections, health and happiness. And so we give very special gifts to the magickal child of light at his or her blessing ceremonies.

Magickal Blessings Quilt

A little quilt made with love makes the perfect baby gift. Infants are particularly open to the energies around them, so it is important that we surround them with love and shield them from potentially damaging energies. Weave a little magick into your quilt and enfold the darling newborn in love and protection.

Materials

- eight 5-inch squares of paper
- 100-percent cotton quilt padding
- sewing needle
- thread
- scissors

- pen
- paper
- pins
- optional: single-fold bias tape
- six 12 inch by 18 inch (quarter flats) cotton fabric plus backing fabric

1. Use the paper squares to make 8 cut-out templates of your chosen magickal symbols.

2. Cut 2 patterned and 2 plain quarter flat pieces of fabric into four 6-inch squares.

3. Arrange the 16 squares in 4 rows of 4. Lay the cut-out paper templates on top of the plain squares to get a feel for the finished design.

4. Once you are happy with the arrangement, make a quick sketch of it for easy reference.

5. Pin the paper templates on the remaining fabric and cut out the symbols.

6. Pin each fabric symbol in place on one of the plain squares of fabric. Use a straight stitch with a ¼-inch hem to sew the symbols in place. The edges will fray slightly, giving a soft edge.

7. With right sides together, pin each row of squares together along the adjoining edges.

8. Sew along the pinned edges with a ½-inch hem.

9. With right sides together, pin each row of squares along the adjoining edges. Sew along the pinned edges of each row of squares.

10. Cut the backing material 12 inches wider and 12 inches longer than the finished patchwork.

11. Cut the quilt padding 5 inches wider and 5 inches longer than the finished patchwork.

12. With wrong sides together, fold and iron a straight, 1-inch border around the edge of the backing material.

13. Lay the backing material face-down on a flat surface. Lay the quilt padding in the center of the backing material. Lay the finished patch work face-up in the center of the quilting.

14. Fold the ironed edge of the backing material over the patchwork top. Pin the folded fabric in place 1 inch from the edge of the patchwork top, making a 3-inch border around the patchwork.

15. Sew the folded edges into place through all the layers of fabric.

16. Add single-fold bias tape over the stitch line for a decorative effect, if desired.

Blessing Milagros

Meaning "miracle," milagros are small religious charms that are used as offerings at sacred sites and as talismans that are carried for healing, blessings, or protection. In many traditional Hispanic homes, these are nailed to the home retablo (see Chapter 4). The meanings of these charms vary according to the individual. A heart-shaped milagro may represent the desire for true love or it may be a request for emotional healing or physical healing of the heart. You may want something symbolic such as this or you may prefer a religious symbol or image of a spirit guide. Whatever you choose, it should represent the blessings you hope will be bestowed upon the little one in your life.

Materials	
• scissors	• marker
• dull pencil with eraser	• tape
• paper	• optional: nail and hammer or string
• ballpoint pen	• soft aluminum or copper craft sheet, 36-gauge
• small popsicle stick	• optional: craft knife

1. Draw your design on the paper and cut out the outline. You may want to leave a tab at the top for of the design for nailing to a retablo or hanging in a baby's room.

2. Trace the outline with a marker and cut it out of the metal. Use caution when working with metal sheets. Though not as sharp as cut aluminum flashing, rough edges can be surprisingly sharp.

3. Tape the paper to the metal and use this as a template to create the inner designs of your milagro.

4. Gently using the popsicle stick, dull pencil, and pen, impress the lines on the paper into the metal. When you have the basic design imprinted in the metal, you may discard the paper and continue to deepen or widen the lines as you wish. Use the popsicle stick to smooth out the edges of the milagro.

5. If you plan to hang the milagro, use the craft knife to cut a small hole in the image or the tab large enough for a nail or string to pass through. Use the popsicle stick to smooth any rough edges.

6. Hold this milagro between both hands and focus your thoughts on the blessings you wish for this child. Imagine those blessings filling this metal and carrying that intent to the child.

7. Loop a string through the hole and hang it out of reach of children, nail it to the family retablo, or give it as a gift to be placed on a family altar.

Birthdays

Kristin's family celebrates Birthday Week, unless it is a decade birthday, then they celebrate Birthday Month. We highly recommend the practice. It is truly great fun!

Your birthday is a celebration of You. It honors the fact that you are here, that you chose to incarnate in this world, and that you are a part of this family and this community. It should be extra special each and every year. And extra special does not mean extra expensive. While digital cameras and trips to the islands are fabulous gifts, the gifts that really touch your heart and carry the energy of love throughout your year are the ones that take more thought than money. The ones that come from caring, particularly the handcrafted ones, are the gifts you remember and keep forever.

Birthday Cards

Greeting cards, and the words within, can be a real treasure. There is something extra special about receiving a handmade card. Liz makes a cartoon image of her family for Yule each year, and friends and family members treasure these little cards. Homemade cards can be drawn, painted, stenciled, block-printed, and even cross-stitched. They may contain photographs, collages, paper folds, paper cuts, and more. See the right side of our cover for ideas on goddess and zodiac cards.

Birthdays are a particularly nice time for making cards because you get to focus on one person without having to make multiple cards. Carve a stamp of a friend's astrological sign, then make one card from it. Give your friend both the card and stamp as a birthday gift. To make multiple cards, try block printing (see God and Goddess Flags in Chapter 5).

Materials

- 12 inch by 6 inch black cardstock paper
- glue stick
- compass
- protractor
- ruler
- pencil
- craft knife
- gold or silver gel pen
- tissue paper (red, yellow, blue, green, purple, and silver)

1. Fold the piece of black cardstock paper in half to make a 6-inch square card.

2. Find the exact center of the square and use a compass to draw a 6-inch wide circle on the card. Cut the circle out, leaving a 1-inch hinge of paper at the top.

3. Draw 3 more circles on the inside of the card: ¼ inch from the edge, ¾ inch from the edge, and 2 inches from the edge of the card.

4. Starting at the top point of the ¼-inch and 2-inch circles only, mark 5 evenly spaced points around the perimeter at 72 degree intervals. Use these points and a ruler to draw the pentagram star. For this card, the pentacle shape remains black and forms the frame of the card.

5. Use a craft knife to cut out the spaces between the lines of the pentacle shape.

6. Cut pieces of colored tissue paper slightly larger than each hole and glue them onto the back of the pentacle frame, covering each hole to make the card look as though it's a stained glass window.

7. Write your message with a gold or silver gel pen, then wait for the glue to dry before closing the card.

Astrological Gift Box

These charming treasure boxes were designed especially for birthdays. Adorned with an astrological symbol and filled with a birthstone or two, they are guaranteed to delight your birthday friend. See one topped with the dancing cranes of peace and long life on the bottom of our cover and another with the red and Ram of Aries at the top right.

Materials

- corrugated cardboard
- scissors
- empty cereal box
- masking tape
- ruler or tape measure
- craft knife
- plastic cloth
- an old phone directory or newspaper
- craft glue
- water
- decorative string
- white gesso
- acrylic paint
- paintbrush
- small dry sea sponge
- super glue
- marble
- birthstone (see the table on page 188)

1. Cut out one 3-inch circle from corrugated cardboard. Cut a strip, 9½ inches long and 2 inches wide from an empty cereal box.

2. Curl the strip into a ring and tape the ends together with masking tape. Place the ring over the circular base and tape them together with small squares of masking tape.

3. To make the box lid, cut two 3¼-inch circles from corrugated cardboard. Use a craft knife to cut a 2½-inch circle from the center of one 3¼-inch circle. Tape the 2½-inch circle to the bottom of the full circle. Tape the 3¼-inch ring to the top of the full circle.

4. Cover your work surface with a plastic cloth. Tear thin strips of paper from an old phone directory or newspaper.

5. Mix white craft glue with equal amounts of water. Dip 1 strip of paper at a time into the paste. Using your fingers to wipe off the excess paste, stick a smooth even layer of paper strips all over the box and lid. Allow this first layer to dry before applying 2 additional layers of papier-mâché.

6. Glue small pieces of string onto the lid in the shape of an astrological symbol. Add decorative string around the edge of the box.

7. When the box and lid are dry, paint them with an undercoat of white gesso acrylic paint.

8. For a rustic-looking box, first paint the box and lid black or dark brown. Then dab a small dry sea sponge in metallic bronze acrylic paint and rub a thin uneven layer of the shiny bronze paint over the box and lid.

9. For a blue and gold box, as shown on our cover, first paint the box and lid dark blue. Let the paint dry, then dip a small paintbrush in metallic silver paint. Hold the brush over the box and tap the handle of the brush so that specks of silver splatter over the box, splatter with gold in the same manner. Highlight the string symbol and lid rim in gold.

10. Mark out an equal-sided triangle on the bottom of the box and superglue a marble at each point to give your box a fancy set of tripod legs.

11. Pop a birthstone or two in the box for your special birthday friend.

Birthstones			
January	garnet	July	ruby
February	amethyst	August	peridot
March	aquamarine, bloodstone	September	sapphire
April	diamond, white sapphire	October	opal, tourmaline
May	emerald	November	topaz, citrine
June	pearl, moonstone	December	turquoise, zircon

Coming of Age

One day, your little girl or boy will become an adult. Hormones will rage, bodies will change, and a transformation takes place right before your eyes. In modern society, this transformation is largely overlooked. What's more, our young people often don't know quite when they qualify as "adults." They can vote or go to war at 18 but they can't drink alcohol until they are 21 in most places. In some areas, they can get married at 15 but they cannot legally own a car or a home until they are 18. It is a very confusing time to be a teen.

But we all know it in our hearts. Puberty is the line for young adults. Once a girl begins to menstruate and a boy ejaculates his first seed, he or she is physically an adult. Hopefully, their friends and families have prepared them mentally and emotionally to handle this change with wisdom and respect. Rites of passage, celebrations, and special gifts all contribute to the empowering transformation that happens at this time.

Stone Dagger

In many cultures, the gift of a special knife is a mark of adulthood. It signifies the knowledge, understanding, and maturity to properly use such a magickal tool. This is not a toy for children but a truly powerful tool for the young man or woman. See one of Kristin's stone daggers in the composite photo on the cover of this book. She chose to spiral gold wire up a black handle to bring out the incredible golds and blacks of the particular piece of stone. To present a hand-carved stone dagger at an adulthood ceremony speaks volumes of your respect and admiration for your beloved young person.

Materials

- soapstone
- small sledge hammer or wooden mallet
- small metal chisel
- metal file or Dremel tool
- pocket knife
- leather gloves
- acrylic coating
- wooden dowel or natural stick
- wood glue
- lint-free cloth
- decorations: leather, feathers, beads, stones, etc.

1. Soapstone is an extremely soft stone found in most art stores. It can easily be carved with a pocket knife but first you will need to rough out the shape of your knife from the block of stone. Using the hammer and chisel, carve out a rectangle or oval at least twice as large as you want your knife blade to be. This is because soapstone flakes off so easily and you do not want to accidentally chisel off half your blade. Test the stone first to see which direction it flakes off and work with that direction when roughing out your blade.

2. Once you have a shape twice as large as your intended blade, carve the blade outline in the soapstone and use the metal file or Dremel to shape the basic outline of the blade.

3. Fine-tune the blade with your pocket knife, using it both as a file and cutting edge. Be very careful, wear gloves to protect your hands, and gently work the knife over the surface as you thin the blade. If you are very careful, you can get the blade to be less than ¼ inch thick, if desired. Keep the base of the blade, where it will attach to the handle, between ¾ inch and 1 inch wide.

4. Run the blade under water to wash off any remaining dust and allow to dry completely.

5. Cut the dowel or stick to the length you desire for your knife handle. If you want to carve a design into the handle, do this now. A spiral running up around the length or yin/yang and peace signs are nice additions.

6. If you want to attach small stone cabochons, carve out shallow depressions and glue them in place now.

7. Leaving ⅛–¼ inch around the outer edge of the stick, Dremel or carve a thin slit in the wood, just large enough for your blade to fit snugly into the wood.

8. Fill the opening with wood glue and insert your blade, wiping off any excess glue with a lint-free cloth. Hold it in position until the glue sets slightly and it does not fall out of place. Prop it up so that it remains in position until the glue is fully dry, at least overnight.

9. Apply 2–3 coats of acrylic coating to bring out the colors and shine as well as to prevent the stone from chipping.

10. Finish adding any decorations to the handle.

Fetish

A fetish is a symbolic representation of a spirit animal. Fetishes are believed to convey the blessings and energies of the spirit ally to the keeper of the fetish. As our children move into the largely unknown territory of adulthood, they are greatly in need of spiritual guidance to help them avoid the pitfalls of modern society and find a path of joy and honor. If you do not know what spirit animal the young adult works with, or if he or she does not recognize one, offer a blessing from your heart, perhaps a bluebird for happiness, a bear for strength, or a turtle for long life. A fetish may also be crafted of clay or soapstone, but in this section we present you with a more durable version, inspired by our friend and wonderful craftsman, Otis.

Materials

- pencil
- scrap paper
- waxed string or sinew
- tracing paper
- wood glue
- wood carving knife
- newspapers
- vise or stack of heavy books
- Dremel or other rotary tool with sanding bit
- sandpaper
- shellac or acrylic coating
- small stone or arrowhead
- optional: feather or beads
- optional: wood stain or paint
- 8–10 sheets of 4 inch by 4 inch wood, 1/10- to ¼-inch wide

1. Sketch a simple fetish design of your animal on scrap paper. When you have it the way you want it, transfer the outline to the tracing paper and from there onto each sheet of wood. When choosing your wood, consider whether or not you plan to paint your fetish. If you will not be painting it, choose wood that is a rich color; perhaps 4 sheets would be pleasing in a lighter shade of the same color.

2. Cut the outline from each sheet of wood. Don't worry too much at this point about making each outline an exact copy of the others. If it is close, you will have the chance to even them all up later on.

3. Separate the sheets into 2 halves. Glue the 4 or 5 of each half together, all facing the same way, and clamp them tightly with a vise or place under a stack of very heavy books until the glue dries completely. You are making a sandwich of wood pieces to create a thicker version of your outline.

4. Glue the 2 halves together and clamp them tightly with a vise or place under a stack of very heavy books until the glue dries completely.

5. Using sandpaper and the Dremel, round the edges and smooth out the outlines. If anything does not match up perfectly, now is the time to even up all edges and make any adjustments to the outline.

6. If you plan to stain or paint the wood, do so now and allow it to dry completely.

7. Cover with 3 coats of shellac or acrylic coating. Allow it to dry completely.

8. Holding the stone or arrowhead in place on the back of the animal, wrap the waxed string or sinew around it tightly and tie off with a small knot at the bottom of the fetish. If you want to include beads or feathers, add them now.

Menarche

The arrival of a young woman's menstrual cycle is huge event in her life. If friends and family do not simply allow society and media commercials to dictate her experience, this can be a truly empowering occasion that she will remember with joy as she ages. To do that requires a great deal of respect, flexibility, and a willingness to honestly honor this phase each month.

Herbal Face Mask

Once menarche arrives, your little girl becomes a woman. This is a truly incredible transition that brings with it some uncomfortable body changes, including acne. This wonderful face mask will make your young woman feel as if she's a pampered queen as it cleanses her face to help prevent pimples.

Materials

- glass or stoneware mixing bowl
- ½ cup oatmeal
- 1 teaspoon chamomile
- ½ teaspoon lemon peel, grated
- 1 tablespoon honey, preferably local
- ½ cup water
- optional: small jar and card

1. In the bowl, combine oatmeal, chamomile, and lemon peel. Mix well. If you are giving this as a gift, pour this mixture into a small jar with the following directions to go along with it. You might also want to give the young woman a small container of local honey.

2. Add the honey to the oatmeal, chamomile, and lemon peel. Mix well.

3. Mix in the water, a little at a time, until it reaches a paste-like consistency.

4. Apply to face. Leave on till dry. Wash off with warm water.

Moontime Healing Kit

Honoring menstrual periods can go a long way to easing the discomforts that can accompany it. This is a powerful time in a woman's life, and your young lady should be encouraged to use this time for visioning, drumming, or meditation. But even with regular moderate exercise and cutting back on foods containing salt, caffeine, and sugar, women may still have unpleasant symptoms during Moontime. This is where the healing kit comes in. Package all or some of the following remedies into a beautiful gift box for the new woman in your life and she will thank you every single month!

Vitamins

- magnesium
- B complex, especially niacin/B6
- vitamin C with bioflavonoids

Homeopathic Remedies

- For pain: Magnesia phosphorica, Colocynthis, Apis mellifica, and Belladonna

- For irritability: Chamomilla and Nux vomica

Herbs for Teas

- dandelion

- dong quai

- red raspberry leaf

- squaw vine

- true cramp bark

- valerian

Manhood

When does a boy become a man? Is it when he turns 13 or 18? When he begins to grow facial hair? When his voice starts to change? Or is it when he produces his first "seed"? There is no standard answer for this, so it will be up to your family to decide.

Whatever you decide, becoming a man is a very big deal. Suddenly, he is no longer simply a boy. He has joined the brotherhood of Men. Admission into that society brings with it certain rights and responsibilities. And it brings with it a need for certain tools and symbols of Manhood. We offer you two suggestions to honor his passage and provide him with some special, yet necessary, tools.

Shaving Soother Tonic

Your young man has reached that point. And just yesterday, he was bouncing on your lap. But now he's shaving and on his way to becoming a man in this world. This shaving tonic is a special gift to acknowledge and honor the changes in his body. You might want to give him the option of splashing it or spraying it on by buying plastic bottles with sprayer tops. And be sure to tell him one the greatest of the men's mysteries: If he microwaves his shaving cream for 30 seconds on medium (in a non-metallic container), he will have a close equivalent to the barbershop hot shave. A real luxury!

Materials

- glass or stoneware mixing bowl
- 3 cups witch hazel
- 2 tablespoons peppermint oil
- 1 teaspoon lavender oil
- flour sifter
- glass or plastic bottles
- stick-on labels
- gift box

1. In your mixing bowl, blend witch hazel, peppermint oil, and lavender oil well.

2. Strain out the herbs with a flour sifter and pour into bottles. Add a label and wrap it up in a handsome box.

Bamboo Didgeridoo

Played by one man while others chant and rhythmically tap sticks and boomerangs around the light of a fire, the didgeridoo is an important part of the Australian Aboriginal ritual of male initiation and the passing on of traditional laws and wisdom. The earthy rhythm and eerie sound of the didgeridoo is often used for trance and meditation. It blends perfectly within the beat of a drumming circle and is ideal for use in manhood ceremonies.

Possibly the oldest wind instrument on earth, the didgeridoo is traditionally made from a sapling or branch of eucalyptus tree that has been hollowed out by termites. But we prefer bamboo, an extremely versatile member of the grass family, for its beauty and because it is a rapidly renewable resource. But keep in mind that bamboo is sensitive to heat and humidity. To prevent cracking, do not expose your didgeridoo to extreme temperature change or direct heat.

Materials

- damp sponge
- rebar, 2–3 feet long
- wood or metal file
- sandpaper
- propane torch
- optional: wood-burning tool
- optional: clear wood finish

- beeswax
- clean, empty tin
- shallow pan of water
- optional: guitar tuner
- a straight piece of bamboo with no cracks, 4 feet long and 2 inches wide, preferably wider at one end

1. Clean your bamboo stick with a damp sponge.

2. Ram a long piece of rebar down into the bamboo, forcefully breaking through the internal membranes that intermittently bridge the inside of the bamboo shaft.

3. To tune your didgeridoo, file down the bell (bottom or widest) end a little at a time and check the pitch with a guitar tuner. The longer the didgeridoo, the lower the pitch will be.

4. Smooth down both ends of the bamboo with sandpaper.

5. For a darker wood color, gently brush the whole surface with the heat of a propane torch. You only want to singe the bamboo, not burn it, so hold the flame about 2 inches from the bamboo and keep it moving.

   NOTE: Read all manufacturer's directions carefully before using a propane torch. Use it in a well-ventilated area away from flammable materials. Never point a torch toward yourself or anyone else.

6. Decorate your didgeridoo with your animal totem or magickal symbols using a wood-burning tool.

7. Give the bamboo a protective finish with a few coats of clear wood finish.

8. Melt some beeswax in a clean, empty tin. Put the can in a shallow pan of water and gently heat the water until the wax has melted.

9. Form a wax mouthpiece by dipping the narrow end of your didgeridoo 1 inch down into the melted wax. Add several more layers of wax. If the second layer of wax melts off the first layer, the wax is too hot. If the wax layers are thick and lumpy or crack, the wax is too cool.

10. While the wax is still warm (not hot), manipulate the shape of the mouthpiece to fit your mouth comfortably.

11. Allow the wax to cool completely. Play, have fun, and don't forget to breathe!

Playing the didgeridoo can be a simple as blowing a raspberry or as complex as circular breathing.

Drone. To make the basic drone sound, gently press your mouth into the wax mouthpiece, relax your whole face, and softly blow through loose lips, allowing your lips to vibrate down into the didgeridoo.

Vocal Projection. Once you have mastered the drone, add vocals to your playing by projecting your voice down the didgeridoo as you drone. A crow's caw or owl hoot are good sounds to start with.

Rhythm and Breath. When playing didgeridoo, time the pause of sound that happens with the intake of your breath to be part of the rhythms you play.

Circular Breathing. Using circular breathing while playing a didgeridoo allows you to make an uninterrupted drone sound. The trick is to fill your cheeks with the air from your lungs. Then refill your lungs with air taken in through your nose while you gently blow out the air stored in your cheeks. Refill your cheeks and repeat. Practice circular breathing by blowing bubbles into a glass of water through a drinking straw. Successful circular breathing will enable you to blow a constant stream of bubbles.

Weddings

The union of two lives—body, mind, and soul—is a profoundly beautiful point in time. Two lovers have chosen to make their commitment a long-lasting one. This demands gifts that commemorate the perfect love and trust that a wedding requires, as well as the fun of it.

Bonding Chalice

In many cultures, the happy couple drinks from a shared cup during the wedding ritual. This signifies their union and the sharing of their lives from that point forward. Though the chalice you give them may or may not be used in the ceremony, this unique cup is sure to be a gift they will love forever.

Materials

- glass vase with an extra wide mouth
- paper and pencil
- craft glue
- at least 1 photo of the couple
- real or faux rose petals
- acrylic coating
- optional: charms, paper hearts, glitter, feathers, leaves, etc.

1. Plan the design for your chalice on a piece of paper. Start with one central photo of the couple and work your way out around the vase-chalice. The idea is to create a memorial to the joy and love shared by this couple.

2. Using a small amount of craft glue, attach the photo to the center of the vase. Continue to glue on the hearts, petals, and other decorations, using only enough glue to get them to stick in place.

3. Allow the glue to dry overnight.

4. Spray with 2 coats of acrylic coating.

Love in a Bottle

Although this can be used for nearly anything, it is a wonderful gift for newlyweds. Spray a little on the wedding bed and allow the aromas to fill your senses, lulling you into happy, loving feelings as you cuddle in the arms of your beloved. Renew this feeling each night or once a week by spraying your pillowcases before bed.

Materials

- ½ cup distilled water
- 8–10 drops each of essential oils of lavender or rose and vanilla
- ½-cup size dark glass bottle with spray top

1. Fill the bottle with distilled water.
2. Add 8–10 drops each of lavender or rose and vanilla essential oils.
3. Screw on spray top and invert bottle 3 times to mix.

Housewarming

The idea behind housewarming gifts is to make the house feel more like "home" and to bring personal and comforting elements into a new house. To help you and your friends create a positive and healthy energy in your new homes, we offer you these crafts that can be used in different areas, new homes, and for unique purposes over time—truly gifts that keep on giving.

House Clearing Kit

Throughout the world, cultures have created methods for clearing out unwanted energies and attracting beneficial energies to human-occupied spaces. This is the perfect housewarming gift to help your friends and family purify their new space and make it really their own.

Into a special box or basket, pack the following items in beautiful tissue paper:

- blessed water
- sea salt
- bowl for water
- flower or small evergreen branch
- matches or lighter
- directions for clearing
- fireproof container
- loose herbs or smudge stick (We recommend sagebrush, cedar, or juniper mixed with lavender or sweetgrass.)

To prepare blessed water, use a cup of spring water, rain water, or other naturally collected water. If this is not possible, tap water is perfectly acceptable.

Take a small amount of sacred herbs, such as the ones you use in smudging, and sprinkle them over the surface of the water. Ask that the sacred herbs clear and purify this water of all unwanted energies and influences that it might be a pure channel for purification and blessings.

Place 1 cup of water in a glass, stone, or pottery container. Hold it between your hands just above eye level. Visualize the purification and blessings you hope for this home and those living in it and send the energy through your hands and "third eye" chakra into the water.

Lower the cup. Take a deep breath and hold your healing intention as you hold your breath. Release this intention to the water and you blow it out onto the surface of the water with your breath.

Directions for House Clearing

1. Light your smudge and ask that the spirits of the sacred herbs cleanse away any unwanted energies, releasing them to the universe. Walk slowly throughout the house, allowing the smoke to penetrate every corner, every doorway, every closet. Be sure to smudge vents, under beds, and around windows. As you go, state your intent to purify this space and allow in only the most beneficial energies:

   By fire and air, do I consecrate and bless this space.

2. Add a pinch of sea salt to your blessed water. Using the flower or evergreen branch, sprinkle the home with this salt water and say:

   By water and earth do I consecrate and bless this space.

3. For added protection against unwanted energies, you might want to do a final round, placing a thin line of sea salt on each doorstep and windowsill. Say:

   Salt of our beginnings, salt of our blood,
   Purify and protect this space against all unwanted energies
   and beings.

Magickal House Scroll

Inspired by the mezuzahs found on the doorposts of many Jewish homes, this magickal house scroll will protect your home with its words and remind you to welcome beneficial, loving energy in to your life. The traditional mezuzah is a scroll of parchment with two perfectly inscribed chapters of the Torah written in Hebrew. The mezuzah scroll is placed in a small box and hung on the right-hand doorpost of an entryway. The power of the written word makes a potent spell, so chose your words carefully and welcome loving energy in to your home with the words you write on to your magickal mezuzah scroll. Here's an example:

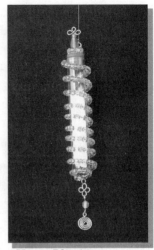

House Blessing

> *May peace prevail in my heart,*
> *May peace prevail in our home,*
> *May peace prevail on Earth.*

Materials

- 4-inch test tube
- 20-gauge wire
- beads
- needle-nose pliers
- super glue

1. Twist a small loop into one end of a 26-inch piece of 20-gauge wire.

2. Spiral loops of wire around the body of the test tube to make a spiraling coil shape.

3. Thread beads onto the wire until the coil is completely covered with beads.

4. Finish off the beaded spiral with a second small loop of wire.

5. Place the test tube inside the beaded spiral then tighten the bottom loop of the coil so that it makes a floor that holds the tube in place when it hangs vertically. Stretch out the coil to cover the length of the tube.

6. Twist a 2-inch length of wire into 4 small loops to make a little 4-leaf clover. Hang the clover from the bottom loop of the beaded coil.

7. Use a small piece of wire to add a bead and a small spiral of wire to the bottom loop of the clover.

8. Glue some beads and a little twist of wire onto the test-tube lid for decoration.

9. Cut and roll a strip of paper to fit inside the tube. Write out a prayer, poem or spell on the scroll of paper that welcomes loving energy in to your life and home. Roll the scroll and place it in the tube.

10. Use the top loop to hang this magickal house scroll by your front door or other entryway in your home, away from wind and the swing of a door.

Mystical Picture Frames

Photo Frame

How many times have you gone shopping to find that perfect picture frame that would bring out the essence of your new photograph, and just couldn't find one that did it justice? This is even more important when someone moves into a new home. They want to make that new space their own so the decorations need to reflect their spirituality and personal tastes. By personalizing even the picture frames, you can help them do this in beautiful and magickal ways that will make a special photograph or artwork come alive.

The directions given include a 5 inch by 7 inch photo and a 9 inch by 12 inch frameless clip frame. The size of the top two mats are in proportion to the photo and the frame but may be adjusted to accommodate designs and patterns you cut into the mats. The following chart gives approximate sizes of mats to use with standard photo and frame sizes. Note that mat #1 is the same size as the frame and used as the base mat to attach your photo.

Size Chart			
Photo Size	Glass/Mat Size	Cutout for Mat #2	Cutout for Mat #3
4" × 6"	8½" × 11"	5" × 7½"	5½" × 8"
5" × 7"	9" × 12"	6 " × 8½"	6½" × 9"
8" × 10"	12" × 16"	9" × 11½"	9½" × 12"
11" × 14"	16" × 20"	12" × 15½"	12½" × 16"

Materials

- standard size photo or artwork
- craft knife
- cutting mat or surface
- frameless clip frame
- craft glue
- ruler or measuring tape

- 1 sheet mat board, white or off-white
- pencil
- 2 sheets of mat board, colors of your choice
- twine or leather cord and nail
- optional: tracing paper

NOTE: You may substitute a standard photo frame with an aluminum or wood border if you like, or for non-standard sizes you can assemble frame parts that are available at most hobby stores.

NOTE: You may need to purchase full 30 inch by 40 inch sheets of mat board, so planning several similar projects may be cost-effective.

1. Take a moment to consider the picture or photo you will use. What symbols does it evoke? The photo on the cover of this book was taken in Arizona and clearly evokes the Southwest imagery, so we chose the design you see in that frame. The photo on page 200 brings through runic energies of protection, joy, and harmony, as well as some specific ones relating to his association with Thor.

   Keep your symbols relatively simple, but make them fit the picture. Make photo enlargements if necessary. Remember that you can always order one size larger and crop your photos to get the required subject within a standard size.

2. Before purchasing the frame and mat board, design your mats and cutouts and draw them full scale on paper. Once you have settled on a design, you can determine the frame size and the cutout sizes for your mats. First try the sizes listed here and adjust as necessary. The mats for the project shown were adjusted to allow more space for the runes.

   Then consider which colors match the symbols and the colors in the picture best. This will determine the colors of your boards. Do you want to emphasize the green leaves, the blue sky, or the red rocks? Perhaps you want someone's blue eyes or auburn hair to stand out. Choose the main element you want emphasized for the top board and the secondary element color for the bottom board. Once you have selected the colors, you are ready to purchase your frame and mat boards at your local hobby store.

In the photo, we used black and cream to offset the photo itself and to accent Karl's gold earrings. Then a small outline of blue brings out his beautiful eyes. The main orange is not only one of his favorite colors but it also fits the overall colors of the photo well. And we used 2 inset blocks of pale red under the runes, to make them stand out and tie in the red of his shirt.

3. Using your full-scale design, redraw or trace your design on to the mat boards.

4. Carefully cut out your designs and the center pieces with your craft knife.

5. Assemble the mats and make any last-minute adjustments before gluing together.

6. On the off-white base mat board, determine the center point and mark the position of your photo. Then glue them together. Glue on the top 2 mat boards. Apply weight on them and allow to dry.

7. Once dry, you can assemble the frame, glass, and mat boards. Tie a knot into a length of twine or leather cord and string this through the side clips on the back of the frame. Use this to hang the picture on a nail in the wall.

Anniversaries

Anniversaries may not have all the pageantry and excitement of a wedding, but they are at least as important. Once each year, a couple honors their ongoing love and commitment to each other and to the vows they took at their wedding. They have a year, or 10, 20, or 60 years, of history together. They have shared the good times, worked through the challenges, and have emerged with a stronger, happier union. This is the proving of the wedding and it would be a shame not to make each and every anniversary a joyful testament to love and unity.

Memory Book

With all that history together, you probably have photo albums and videos to remember it by. But you'd really need to go through all of them to get a feel for how those events influenced your relationship. They don't show how you felt the moment after the photo was taken or the week after. They don't always help you remember what you said or who else was there or all those little but special things that create a richness of experience. That is where the Memory Book comes in.

This is a book with a purpose. Its focus is to re-create in a tangible way, the life of your relationship. Using colors, textures, and a host of other clever elements, simply flipping through this book will bring back all the memories and feelings of your journey together. And what's even better, you can add to it as the years go by.

Necessary Materials

- pencil and scrap paper
- scissors
- a range of photos covering your life together
- craft glue
- hole punch
- circular book binders
- pens and markers in fun colors
- ruler
- 8½" × 11" light cardboard or heavy paper
- 8½" × 11" cardstock-weight paper

Optional Materials

- clear plastic cabochons
- small envelopes
- red construction or metallic paper
- love notes to each other
- vellum sheet
- watercolor paper
- paintbrush
- watercolor paint and water
- heart-shaped sequins
- heart-shaped plastic cabochons
- strings, fabric pieces, fluffy yarn, colored wire
- a petal from the bride's bouquet
- sewing needle
- metallic red thread
- small pieces from the bride's and groom's (if possible) wedding attire

1. Plan out the book on scrap paper first. Decide how many pages you want for now and make a plan for each page. Plan the cover, front, and back.

   Use the light cardboard or heavy paper for the covers and the other paper or cardstock for the interior pages. Because this is such a unique book, we can't give you a cookbook instruction on how to create it. But we can offer some great ideas.

- Using soft aluminum sheets or a special paper, cut out a picture frame and paste this around a special photo of the happy couple on the cover.

- Borrow the Mystical Picture Frame idea in this chapter to frame a title or photo for your cover.

- Add a small envelope every few pages and put a love note, special poem, or fun "Remember When..." in it.

- Highlight important dates or special words by gluing a clear cabochon over them. This will magnify the word or image beneath it.

- Mix a small amount of your favorite watercolor with a great deal of water. Wash a sheet of watercolor paper with this. When dry, tear it off and glue it to one page of the book. This can frame a photo or make a "journal entry" stand out from the rest of the page.

- Cut red hearts from special paper and glue them throughout the book. Alternate with heart-shaped sequins or heart-shaped plastic cabochons.

- Laminate a single petal from the bride's bouquet and attach that on the inside cover.

- Using metallic red thread, sew pieces of the wedding clothes to the wedding page.

- Keep going. The possibilities are endless!

2. Craft each page separately and allow any glue or paint to dry completely.

3. Once you have all the pages ready to bind, punch 2 or 3 holes at the same point on each page. This is where they will be bound together. It helps to measure with a ruler and mark each hole location so they match up perfectly.

4. Gently place the pages, one on top of the other, in the order you want them. Clip on the book binders and wrap it up in beautiful paper before giving it as a gift.

Photo memory book

Yummy Body Paints

You might think of this more as a wedding or Valentine's Day craft, and it certainly could be. But this kind of fun should not be limited to the honeymoon or the first flush of love. Those of us celebrating our first, 10th, and 50th anniversaries could use something such as this to spice up our private celebrations. And what a fun way to rekindle the romance on your anniversary!

Materials

- ⅓ cup whipping cream
- 3 ounces white chocolate
- small pan
- 5 drops food coloring in various colors
- 1–2 teaspoons syrups in your favorite flavors or flavored liqueurs
- electric mixer
- medium bowl

1. Lightly beat the whipping cream in a medium bowl.
2. Melt the chocolate over medium heat in a small pan.
3. To the whipped cream, add the food coloring and syrup of your choice. Then add the melted chocolate and beat together. Add additional coloring and syrup or liqueur to your liking.
4. Chill in refrigerator for 20 minutes. Remove and beat again until it reaches a thick, spreadable consistency.
5. Play with immediately. If you need to "serve" later, chill it in the refrigerator and add another ½ teaspoon syrup or liqueur before playing with it.

Mother's Day and Father's Day

There is no greater love than that of a parent for a child. Becoming parents changes us forever and hopefully spurs each of us to become better individuals. Let your parents (or grandparents or god/dess parents) know that you appreciate this love and all they do for you, or help your children honor these special days for his or her other parent. Hand-made crafts say it all through the time and thought you put into them. You can be sure that a gift made by a child for a parent will be treasured for life.

Coupon Books

When Kristin was a kid, she loved to give special coupon books as gifts. As a mom, she loves to receive these and still enjoys giving them. The idea behind these little books is to give of yourself, not just to go out and buy a present for Mom or Dad on this special day. Each coupon is for something wonderful: a hug, a kiss, a homemade dinner. Or your coupons may be designed to help take some of the stress off your over-worked mom or dad. Perhaps you will offer coupons for doing the dishes, cleaning the bathroom, or washing a car.

Materials

- 2–3 sheets of cardstock
- scissors
- pens, crayons, colored pencils
- brightly colored ribbon or yarn
- hole punch

1. Cut each sheet of cardstock into 8 equal pieces, 2 inches by 5 inches.

2. Punch a hole in the center of each coupon on the side, about ½ inch from the end. Be sure the holes are lined up so they will attach together as a book.

3. Create a cover for your coupon book with one of the pieces. Include a title, date, and the names of who is giving this gift and who is receiving it.

4. On the front of each of the remaining pieces, draw your coupon with any decorations you would like.

5. When all the coupons are complete, stack them up and string a festive ribbon through the holes. Tie this tight enough to keep them together but loose enough to be able to flip through the pages easily.

Incense Burner

As spiritual parents, we use incense for a variety of things and some-times just because it smells nice. These sweet incense holders are great fun to make and remind us each time we see them of the joy and love that went into their creation. Check out the adorable little dolphin holding incense on the top left of our cover. Notice how the base of the holder evokes the images of sea waves. Young kids may need help with this project, but they are guaranteed to have fun. Moms or dads who are allergic to incense can proudly display this incense burner on their desk and use it to hold a favorite pen.

Materials

- at least 3 ounces of polymer clay (various colors)
- oven and baking sheet
- colored pencils
- paper
- pin

1. Decide what animal and colors you want to use and create a color sketch to use as a guide.

2. Make a marbled tray by mixing together 2 or 3 colors of clay. Mix the colors together until you are satisfied with the overall marble effect.

3. Roll the marbled clay into a 9-inch-long sausage. Flatten the sausage into a long tray shape, about 10 inches long.

4. Use the pad of your thumb to smooth out a shallow channel down the center of the tray or pinch all around the edge of the tray to make a little wavy rim.

5. Draw the animal you wish to make snowman style, using a combination of simple shapes.

6. Using your sketch as a guide, build a small animal from simple shapes of clay. Smooth or gently press each piece together.

7. Make the eyes and other little details from tiny balls of clay. Gently press them into place.

8. Use the point of a pin to scratch in details such as mouth, nostrils, bushy squirrel tail, lion's mane, fish scales, or claws.

9. Attach your little animal to one end of the tray by gently smoothing the clay together. If your animal is sitting up and has arms, wings, or front legs, you can put its paws together in a circle so that there is a space between the body and arms. The animal can then hold the incense stick in this space.

   Alternatively, you can roll a small ball of clay and press it onto the tray close to the animal. Poke a narrow hole, at a 45-degree angle from the tray, into the ball of clay with the wooden end of an incense stick.

10. Put an incense stick in position and adjust the paws or ball until the incense stick rests perfectly in line with the ash-catching tray.

11. Take out the incense stick and bake the incense burner according to the clay manufacturer's directions.

Earth Day

Although many groups celebrate Earth Day on April 22nd of each year, the original, and some say the true, Earth Day occurs on the Spring Equinox because it symbolizes great balance and harmony. Started as a suggestion in San Francisco in 1969 by John McConnell, the Earth Day celebration has grown and spread to countries throughout the world. Each year, on the moment of the Equinox, the Peace Bell is rung at the United Nations headquarters. This bell was made from coins donated by Japanese schoolchildren. The ringing of the Peace Bell is traditionally followed by two minutes of silence.

Candelabra

In the spirit of this balance and beauty, we offer you a candelabras with a spiritual theme often represented by "The Tree of Life." This one was designed for use with the 3 Candles for Peace meditation.

Candleabra

Materials

- wire mesh
- 16-gauge wire
- 26-gauge wire
- 4-inch round wooden base
- wire cutters or scissors
- stapler
- casting plaster
- 4 gauze bandages, each cut into 3-inch strips

- plastic container
- sieve
- stirring spoon
- rasp or metal file
- clay
- acrylic paints
- optional: cookie cutters
- old, dry pen
- all-purpose sealer

NOTE: Work in a well-ventilated area and wear a dust mask and rubber gloves when mixing plaster.

1. Roll a 15 inch by 10 inch rectangle of wire mesh into a 15-inch cone with a 2-inch diameter base and a 1-inch diameter top. Tie the cone in place with 26-gauge wire.

2. Snip six ½-inch vertical slits around the base of the cone. Then splay them out and staple the cone in place on the wooden base.

3. Cut two 24-inch lengths of 16-gauge wire. Attach the wires to the base of the cone directly opposite each other by bending the last inch of wire at a right angle and stapling it to the wooden base. Tie the bottom 4 inches of wire vertically to the side of the central cone with 26-gauge wire.

4. Cut two 16 inch by 10 inch rectangles of wire mesh. Wrap one of these rectangles around each long wire forming a 16-inch cylinder with a 1½-inch diameter.

5. Shape the candelabra arms by bending the mesh-covered wire into a loop at each side of the central cone. Tie the arms in place about 4 inches down from the top of the central cone with the protruding "arm" wire.

6. Make each candleholder cup by folding a 6 inch by 4 inch rectangle of mesh into a 6 inch by 2 inch rectangle and rolling it into a 2-inch-wide circle. Close in 1 end with little folds to make the cup shape. Attach each little cup to the top of the candelabra with wire.

7. Mix the plaster 1 small batch at a time in a plastic container. Sieve 1½ cups of plaster into 1 cup of water. Gently stir the mix together, then give the bowl a little shake to bring any air bubbles to the surface. Flexing the plastic bowl will loosen dry plaster.

8. Working quickly, drench one gauze strip at a time in the plaster then wrap it around the armature. Mix more plaster as needed.

9. Once you have covered the whole candelabra with plastered gauze, mix a new batch of plaster and let it set to the consistency of whipped cream. Then quickly spread it all over the candelabra, covering the gauze and filling gaps with an even layer of plaster. Once the plaster has set, smooth the surface with a rasp.

10. Roll out a ½-inch-thick slab of clay on a smooth, flat surface. With the clay stuck to the work surface, cut out circles for the Earth, Sun, and Moon. Cut out 18 small leaf shapes. Fill the hollow shapes with freshly mixed plaster.

11. When the plaster shapes are dry, remove them from the clay. Smooth edges with a file and carve any details with an old pen.

12. Attach the Sun, Moon, and Earth to the front of the center cone with a blob of plaster.

13. Poke little holes in one end of each leaf and around the outer branches of the candelabra. Connect the leaves to the candelabra by pushing 1-inch bits of wire into the holes. Dab on a little plaster to hold the leaves in place. Use the remaining plaster to cover any tufts of gauze or imperfections.

14. Coat the dry plaster with a layer of all-purpose sealer and finish with a decorative coat of acrylic paint.

3 Candles for Peace

This beautiful exercise was first printed in Llewellyn's *2004 Spell-A-Day Almanac.* Place your candelabra in the center of a table and sprinkle some vervain around it. Place a candle in each of the holders: green, pink, and blue. Say:

> *A green candle is lit for the Earth. May all beings on this planet know healing.*
>
> *A pink candle is lit for love. May all beings on this planet love and feel loved.*
>
> *A blue candle is lit for enlightenment. May all beings on this planet radiate peace and harmony.*

Meditate on the Earth on your candelabra. See love permeate all things of this planet and heal all wounds. Visualize a world that is peaceful and celebrates harmonious diversity.

More Magickal Delicacies

Every holiday needs its own unique foods. The sight, taste, and aroma of celebratory delicacies gives the holidays a luxurious and opulent feel. This separates them from ordinary days and makes everyone involved feel extra special. These offerings may be used for any special occasion and can be slightly adapted to fit each of the holidays in this book.

Divine Cakes

Mmmmm, what is more divine than angel food cake? It is so light and moist and fine that it just melts in your mouth like clouds of the most incredible taste. Add your favorite additions, such as fruit or chocolate, and you will swear you've opened the doors to Divinity. This is the cake to make when you are really celebrating and want everything to be extra special!

Materials

- 2 large bowls
- electric mixer
- flour sifter
- 10 inch by 3¾ inch angel food cake pan
- 12 egg whites
- 1½ teaspoon cream of tartar
- 1½ cups sugar
- 1½ teaspoon pure vanilla extract
- ½ teaspoon pure almond extract

- 1 cup sifted cake flour
- ¼ teaspoon salt
- knife
- metal spatula
- sturdy funnel
- narrow spatula or butter knife
- serving plate
- optional filling: pudding or fruit mixture
- optional topping: frosting, fruit topping, or honeyed whipped cream (from Chapter 8)

Fruit Topping:

2 cans of fruit

2 tablespoons cornstarch

2 tablespoons butter

1 tablespoon lemon juice

½ cup sugar

1. Preheat oven to 375 degrees F.
2. Whip the egg whites and the cream of tartar until it's foamy and stands in soft peaks.
3. Mix in ¾ cup of the sugar, a little at a time. Beat until sugar is dissolved. Test to be sure by rubbing a small amount between your index finger and thumb. It will feel gritty if the sugar is not yet dissolved.
4. Add the vanilla and almond extracts.
5. Sift the flour, remaining sugar, and salt together in another large bowl.

6. Then sift ½ cup of this flour mixture over the egg white mixture. Gently fold it in until flour disappears. Continue this process with the remaining flour mixture, ½ cup at a time.

7. Pour batter into ungreased angel food cake pan. Gently cut through the batter with a metal spatula.

8. Bake 30–40 minutes, until the top springs back when touched.

9. Invert the cake in the pan on a funnel, so that it is suspended above the surface slightly, and allow it to cool for 1½ to 2 hours.

10. When the cake is completely cool, loosen the edges with a narrow spatula or butter knife, then shake carefully onto serving plate.

11. To put a filling inside your cake, cool the cake in a refrigerator while you prepare the filling. This is delicious mixed with chopped strawberries, blueberries, or crushed pineapple. Prepare pudding according to the manufacturer's directions.

12. Cut the cake in half to make an opening for the filling. Carve a shallow trench in both the top and bottom.

13. Add your filling to the bottom trench, piled high. Then replace the top half.

14. Top with frosting, honeyed whipped cream, or this yummy fruit topping:

    In a medium pan, cook the juice of the 2 cans of fruit over medium heat with the cornstarch until thick.

    Add the butter, lemon juice, and sugar and cook until sugar dissolves. This does not need to be as well dissolved as for the cake.

    Cool slightly and mix in the fruit. Top the cake with this mixture and refrigerate until ready to serve.

Gift Chocolates

There is nothing more magickal than handmade chocolates. To craft these delicacies by hand and give them as a gift is to show true love and friendship—and the extra touch of red chili in these chocolates adds an extra dose of joy and satisfaction for those you love. Kristin likes to keep a few of these in the freezer for celebration and for days when someone in the house just needs a little pick-me-up. The men in her house prefer the mint or peanut butter versions. What will your favorite be?

Materials

- small pot
- 5–6 ounces sweet dark or milk baking chocolate
- baker's parchment paper
- cookie tin
- ½ cup heavy cream
- ¼ teaspoon vanilla
- medium bowl
- electric mixer
- small spoon
- butter knife
- 6 paper candy cups or candy cases
- 1 teaspoon mild red chili powder, 2 ounces peanut butter chips, or ½ teaspoon spearmint
- pinch cocoa powder

1. Melt 2½ ounces of chocolate in a small pan over medium heat. Mix frequently. Allow the chocolate to solidify slightly on the bottom of pan, not burning but no longer smooth, creamy chocolate.

2. Using the small spoon or knife, coat the inside of the paper candy cups with the melted chocolate. Be sure to completely cover the bottom of the cup. Be careful and fairly quick when doing this. Melted chocolate is hot and it doesn't remain at that ideal consistency for long in the pan.

3. Turn upside down on parchment paper on the cookie tin and place in the freezer overnight to set the chocolate. Once set, gently tear off the paper cup from the chocolate. You should be left with a chocolate cup.

4. Slightly whip heavy cream. Add remaining chocolate, vanilla, and either red chile, peanut butter chips, or spearmint. Whip until soft peaks form with electric mixer on high.

5. Spoon mixture into chocolate cups. Dust tops with cocoa.

6. Place in refrigerator for at least 1 hour before serving.

Flower Petal Gift Box

As if handmade chocolates were not special enough, here is a beautiful gift box for presenting your chocolates or other small gift. See two of these unique little treasures at the top of our cover.

- box pattern
- colorful cardstock paper
- scissors
- tracing paper
- pencil
- glue
- tissue paper
- optional: ruler

1. Photocopy the box pattern and enlarge it to suit your needs. For example, a 12-inch-wide box pattern works well for a small chocolate box.

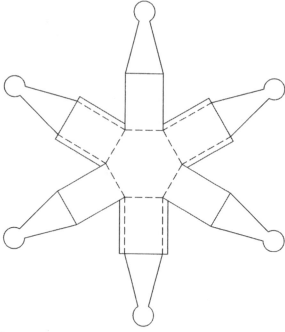

Gift box pattern

2. Trace the box pattern onto a sheet of cardstock paper. Cut out the box shape as precisely as you can.

3. Place the open box face-down on a flat surface. Fold the box upwards or inwards along each fold line. Folding along the straight edge of a ruler will help you make perfect folds.

4. Fold each "petal" up (90 degrees) to form the box shape. Spread a little glue neatly over each tab section. Glue the box together by sticking each tab in place behind its neighboring straight-edged "petal section."

5. Once the glue has dried, your box is ready for stuffing. Wrap a few chocolates loosely inside a square of tissue paper. Place them in the box then scrunch up the tissue paper to fill the inside of the box.

6. Close the box by overlapping the circle-shaped "petal" tips. The circles will lock onto each other if you hook the little cut slash of 1 circle around the un-slashed side of another circle.

This versatile little box can be presented in a number of ways:

- Interlock only each alternate petal tip so that 3 petals point up.
- Interlock as above then close the 3 open petals over the 3 closed petals.
- Interlock the petals in 3 groups of 2.
- Interlock the petals in 2 groups of 3.
- Interlock each neighboring petal to form a top flower.
- Leave the box open to look like a crown.

Goddess Bread

A true celebration of womanhood, this is the perfect addition to any menarche, pregnancy, or Goddess event. The fertile womb of the Goddess is symbolic of the fertile land of the Earth and so it is that the feminine deities of agricultural communities play a significant part in the prayers and ritual for good harvest, fertility, and growth.

Throughout history people of the world have depended on the harvesting of grain for survival and bread has been made in numerous shapes and forms the world over. There is even evidence that some sort of unleavened bread was baked on hot stones as far back as the end of the last ice age!

Materials

- ¼ cup warm water (110 degrees)
- 1 sashay dry active yeast (2¼ teaspoons)
- ⅓ cup warm milk (110 degrees)
- ⅓ cup pure maple syrup
- ½ teaspoon salt
- ¾ cup butter at room temperature
- 6 eggs at room temperature
- 5 cups all-purpose flour
- small towel
- greased baking sheet
- knife
- large bowl
- stirring spoon

1. Pour the warm water into a large bowl. Stir in the yeast until completely dissolved.

2. Mix in the warm milk, maple syrup, salt, and butter.

3. Stir in 5 of the eggs.

4. Gradually fold in about 4½ cups of the flour to make a firm ball of dough. Cover the bowl of dough with a small towel and set it aside to rise in a warm space for 2 hours. The dough should double in size.

5. Knead the dough on a floured surface for about 15 minutes, until the ball of dough is nice and smooth. If the dough is sticky, just add more flour.

6. Put the goddess together on a large non-stick or well-greased baking sheet.

    Cut the dough in half. Use the first half to make a big, flat, upside-down pear shape that will represent the legs and torso of your goddess.

    Divide the second half of the dough into 4 pieces. Roll ¼ into a ball-shaped head. Place the head on the tray at the top of the upside-down pear shape so that the 2 pieces touch each other.

    Cut the second ¼ in half and make 2 balls. Press them on your goddess's chest to form her breasts.

    Cut the third ¼ in 3 and roll out 3 long sausages of dough. Braid the 3 sausages together. To make hair for your goddess, encircle the top of her head with the braid and rest the end of the braid on her shoulders.

    Use 1 half of the last ¼ to make sausage-shaped arms. Push the arms in place and flatten the ends of each arm to make hands.

    Use the remaining dough for eyes, Moon crown, nipples, and any other detail you wish to add. Press all these details gently in place. Use a knife to separate the legs and fingers. Push a hole in to her tummy to give her a belly button.

    Cover the finished Goddess with a small towel and set aside for about 30 minutes to rise.

7. Brush the goddess with the remaining egg and bake in the oven at 350 degrees for 30 minutes.

Shepherd's Pie

Hearty and rich, Shepherd's Pie is the kind of meal a man can truly appreciate. Traditionally made of lamb (hence the name shepherd) and encased in pastry crust, this one-pot wonder is much simpler and can be made from any meat or no meat at all. It is perfect for a manhood celebration. Serve it warm with biscuits to rejuvenate your young man after a quest, ritual, or day of celebrating.

Materials

- 4 large potatoes
- 1 tablespoon butter
- 1½ onions, chopped
- ½ cup shredded cheddar cheese
- salt and pepper to taste
- 5 carrots, chopped
- 1 tablespoon olive oil
- 1 pound beef, lamb, or tofu (ground or cubed)
- 2 tablespoons all-purpose flour
- 1 tablespoon tomato paste
- ¾ cup beef broth
- 2 large pots
- milk for mashing potatoes (approx. ¼ cup)
- electric mixer
- potato peeler
- large frying pan
- 2-quart casserole dish

1. Preheat oven to 375 degrees F.
2. Boil a large pot of salted water. Peel and cube the potatoes then add them to the boiling water for 15 to 20 minutes. Drain the water and mash the potatoes.
3. Add butter, 1 tablespoon onion, and ¼ cup shredded cheese; mix well. Add salt and pepper to taste. Set aside.
4. Boil the carrots for about 15 minutes. Drain the water and mash them. Set aside.
5. In frying pan, sauté the rest of the onion in oil until transparent. Then brown the meat or cook the tofu for 5 minutes.
6. Drain any excess fat and oil. Mix in flour and cook for 1 minute.
7. Add tomato paste and beef broth and bring to a boil. Reduce heat and simmer for 5 minutes.
8. In the casserole dish, layer first the beef/tofu, then the carrots. Then top with mashed potatoes and sprinkle with remaining shredded cheese.
9. Bake 20 minutes until golden brown.

Celebration Fizzies

For a celebration, you can always go out and buy a bottle of sparkling cider or champagne. But isn't it more fun to use those bottles to create something truly special? Of course it is! Try this for your next baby blessing, wedding, or anniversary and see how happy it makes your guests.

Materials

- 1 bottle sparkling cider or champagne
- 1–2 cups fruit juice
- punch bowl
- ice

- optional: ¼ cup blackberry or other brandy, 2 scoops of homemade ice cream (see the next section)
- optional: flower blossoms

1. Pour the champagne or cider and the fruit juice into the punch bowl. Mix well.
2. Add ice and brandy (if desired).
3. Float the blossoms on top and enjoy!

Homemade Ice Cream

Hot days, celebrations, Fridays—all of these have one thing in common: They are all perfect times for ice cream! You need not purchase an expensive ice cream maker to enjoy natural and delicious homemade ice cream. In fact, this can be simple enough even for kids to make, though we do offer you a special kids' version of this magickal delicacy.

Materials

- 2 coffee cans with lids: 1 large and one small
- 3 eggs
- 1 cup whole milk
- 1 cup light cream
- 1 cup sugar

- 1 teaspoon vanilla
- ¼ teaspoon table salt
- crushed ice
- ¾ cup Kosher salt
- optional: fresh crushed fruit
- optional: tape or rubber band

1. Beat the eggs very well until fluffy.
2. Mix in milk, cream, sugar, vanilla, table salt, and fruit.

3. Pour this mixture into the smaller coffee can. Seal the lid securely. You may want to tape or rubber band it to ensure that the lid stays on.

4. Place the smaller can into the larger one. Fill the space around the smaller can about a third of the way up with ice. Sprinkle a layer of Kosher salt on top and add ice another third of the way up. Sprinkle a final layer of Kosher salt on top and top off with ice.

5. Seal the lid to the larger can securely. Shake or roll around for 10 minutes. Remove the lids and check the mixture. If it is not frozen and "ice-creamy," drain any excess water and repack the top layer of ice. Reseal the lids and continue shaking for another 5 to 10 minutes.

   NOTE: You must use extremely fresh eggs for this recipe, no more than 3 days old. Store-bought eggs are **not** recommended. We buy ours from a local organic farm, where we can be assured of proper handling and dates.

Kids' Cream

It doesn't get much easier than this. With adult supervision, even toddlers can make their own ice cream with this recipe.

Materials

- 2 zipper-sealed plastic freezer bags: 1 quart size and 1 sandwich size
- 1 tablespoon sugar
- ½ cup milk
- ½ teaspoon vanilla or flavored syrup
- crushed ice
- 6–7 tablespoons Kosher salt

1. Combine the sugar, milk, and vanilla or syrup in the smaller bag. Press out most of the air and seal.

2. Place a small amount of ice in bottom of larger bag and place the small bag in on top of the ice. Surround the smaller bag with ice to half full.

3. Sprinkle the salt on top of the ice and seal the larger bag.

4. Shake 5–10 minutes until the contents thicken.

Chapter 12

Living a Magickal Life

To live a magickal life is to create each moment consciously, guided by Divine inspiration. Every encounter is recognized as a sacred one. Every situation is perceived as an opportunity for learning and growth. And the potential for joy exists everywhere.

As you open to creativity by crafting the ideas in this book and making them your own, you become a conduit for magick to flow into your life. Simply through being aware of the influx of creativity, you will be more conscious and connected.

But there is more to it than that. That is why we offered you spells, meditations, and other tools for making your creations more magickal. And that is why we added this chapter, with even more ideas to help you integrate the magick of creation into your entire lives.

Intent and Focus

Most people agree that you create your own experience of life. Focus determines that creation. To create what you want, you must set an intent and focus your energy there. Of course, you also need to believe you can do it, but belief develops through success, both small and large.

With that in mind, it can be very important to set an intent for your creations, particularly objects crafted for ritual, sacred space, and divination. This way, your focus is clear each time you use sacred objects and magickal crafts. Dedication rituals are ideal for setting this intent in a sacred and memorable way.

Dedication Ritual

This basic outline is all you need to craft a beautiful and personal rite to dedicate your tools to love, healing, inspiration, or whatever you choose.

This type of ritual is also recommended because it allows you a very special, sacred way of giving thanks to and releasing the spirits of any animals used in crafting your tools. Whether or not you believe the creature's energies are held in its skin, fur, or other parts, this is beneficial because it continues the cycle of appreciation, love, and gratitude that will only further bless your life.

Materials

- the altar of your choosing, set with symbols of your spirit allies and deities
- smudge or incense
- essential oil of myrrh, frankincense, lemongrass, or rosemary

1. Smudge or cense your altar, yourself, your ritual space, and your new tool. Visualize any unwanted energies breaking up and releasing from your tool.

2. Invite in your spirit guides, patron deities, and any other beings you wish to have present. Ask the guidance and protection of these beings during this ritual and beyond. Then state the purpose of this rite:

   Honored spirits, I come before you to present my newly crafted _____(name/type of tool),

   Please bless this tool and the work we will do together.

   I dedicate this _____ (name/type of tool) *to the highest good.*

   I ask that only the most beneficial energies may flow through each of us

   May our every action honor you.

3. Hold the purified tool in both hands and visualize it filling with light and pure energy. Imagine your energy filling it and a connection forming between the two of you, so you might use it to its greatest benefit.

4. Take up the essential oil and hold it between both hands. Offer it to those invoked and ask for their blessings. Anoint yourself with the oil, blessing yourself with the qualities you want to bring to your path. Then anoint the tool, blessing it with the intent you created it for.

   Sit with your tool for a few moments to allow any spirit messages to come through.

5. Thank and release all spirits you invited to join in this ritual.

6. Close sacred space and keep your tool in a safe and special place.

Keep the Magick Flowing

Sometimes you can get so busy that you put off any form of magick, ritual, or meditation. You think to yourself, "I'll do it tomorrow (or next week)," and the next thing you know months have gone by. You stop to think when the last time you connected with your own creativity or your spiritual path in a concrete way was, and you can't remember. What you may notice is a tightness in your shoulders or the fact that you haven't taken a nice deep breath lately either. You've been overtaken by stress and that endless list of things you need to do.

Maintaining a spiritual practice in some form greatly reduces stress. It makes us healthier and happier people, better able to give to the world and to create the lives we want. So it's important to ensure that you keep those creative, spiritual juices flowing. But how do you do that without giving something else up?

First, you recognize that you are at least as important as that to-do list. What's more, you will do all those things more effectively and efficiently if you take care of yourself and have some fun, too. If you have this book, you enjoy making things. So make an appointment for your creativity to flow freely!

- Get out your calendar and a glitter marker in your favorite color.

- Pick one day each week (or each month if you feel pressured to do it every week) to use 30 minutes to do something creative.

- Don't just circle that day; decorate it and make it stand out as something fun.

- Now make 2 lists of ideas: Quickies and Big Projects. Quickies are just that: quick and easy crafts you can make or spells, visualizations, and so forth that you can do in 30 minutes or less. Big Projects are the ones you commit to for a longer period of time. These can last anywhere from one hour to several weeks.

- Post the lists beside your calendar and use them to decide what you will do each time that day comes around.

- If the day arrives and you are honestly tired or can't make the time until late at night, whip up a simple Magickal Delicacy, light a homemade candle, and take a relaxing bath with your favorite bath salt.

- On days when you find you have extra time, make up a few extra delights for the days you are stressed or pressed for time, perhaps a few extra chocolates, some soap and candles, incense, and of course some body oil for those times when you can enjoy a friendly massage.

Creating magick in your life has a way of spilling over into the world at large. People living magickal lives tend to want to spread that joy around and continue the cycle of happiness so that others might feel the same way. There are as many ways to do this as there are people in this world. You might choose to craft beautiful gifts to give away or elaborate ritual tools to use in public rituals. Perhaps you prefer to make drums and rattles to take to a drumming circles for those that have none. Or maybe your way is completely different.

We have a suggestion for you that not only allows your own creativity to flow in a balanced and peaceful way, but it also provides a unique opportunity to do something really big.

Peace Cranes

Before paper became mass-produced, paper-making was a skilled craft. As a result, every sheet of paper was treasured. In the Orient, origami (folded paper) was used to craft a variety of powerful images. These precious gifts were given as offerings to deities in Buddhist shrines.

Traditionally the crane symbolizes peace, long life, and prosperity. According to Japanese legend, the elegant crane lives for 1,000 years. Folding 1,000 paper cranes will grant a wish and ensure long healthy life.

In August 1945, Sadako Sasaki was just 2 years old when her home city of Hiroshima, Japan, was devastated by the first atomic bomb ever used in war. World War II ended soon after the bomb, but many people died from the aftereffects of radiation. Ten years after the bomb, Sadako was diagnosed with radiation sickness and leukemia.

Encouraged by her best friend, Sadako folded more than 1,000 origami cranes with her wish to run and be well again. Twelve-year-old Sadako died in 1955, but her spirit lives on, spreading peace across the world.

Peace Crane Pattern

Colored side of paper	Blank side of paper	Fold direction	Unfold	Fold & unfold	Flip paper over	Turn + degree	Reference point

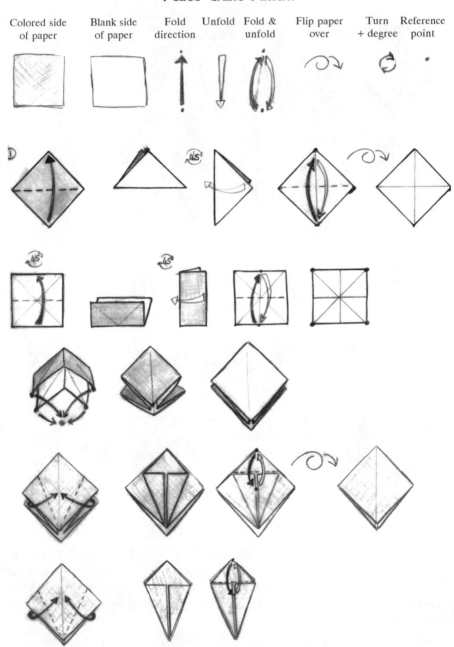

Peace Crane Pattern (continued)

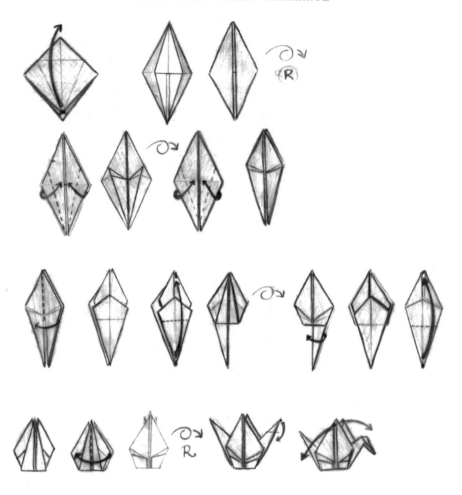

Friends of Sadako were so moved by her story that they published a book of her letters and started raising money to build the Sadako statue that now stands in the Hiroshima Peace Park. The Peace Park stands on the spot where the bomb fell. Sadako's statue stands tall, holding a golden crane as a tribute to all the children that were killed by the bomb and a plea for peace.

Origami cranes have become a universal symbol of peace. People from all over the world fold cranes and display them as a declaration of peace. Teachers and humanitarians use them with Sadako's story to spread the message of peace. Liz led our Peace Pals group through the process, and even our little ones were crafting their own peace cranes by the end. See two of our creations on the right side of the cover of this book.

Though it may sound complicated, with a little practice you can learn to make your own peace cranes and teach others to make them. Follow the pattern on pages 225 and 226 to craft your own cranes. When choosing paper for this project, keep in mind that larger cranes are easier to make in the beginning.

Materials

- origami paper

- optional: strings for holding several cranes together

To make a big statement about the value of peace, and bring the energy of peace into your own life, take this a step further, as so many people around the world have done. Thread 100 cranes on a single thread, then make 10 more of those threads and send your 1,000 cranes of peace to Hiroshima's Peace Park.

Send your cranes to:

> Office of the Mayor
> City of Hiroshima
> 6-34 KoKutaiji-Machi
> 1 Chome Naka-Ku,Hiroshima 730
> Japan

May magick fill your life and may peace prevail throughout the world.

Kristin and Liz

References and Recommended Reading

Spiritual/Magickal

Biedermann, Hans. *Dictionary of Symbolism.* New York: Meridian, Penguin Books. 1994.

Bowes, Susan. *Life Magic.* New York: Simon & Schuster, 1999.

Cunningham, Scott. *Cunningham's Encyclopedia of Magical Herbs.* St. Paul, Minn.: Llewellyn Publications, 1993.

Ford, Patrick K. (ed., transl.) *The Mabinogi and Other Medieval Welsh Tales.* Berkeley and Los Angeles: University of California Press, 1977.

Freeman, Mara. *Kindling the Celtic Spirit.* New York: HarperCollins, 2001.

Gifford, Jane. *The Wisdom of Trees.* New York: Sterling Publishing Company, 2001.

Guiley, Rosemary Ellen. *The Encyclopedia of Witches & Witchcraft.* New York: Checkmark Books, 1999.

Johnson, Cait, and Maura D. Shaw. *Celebrating The Great Mother.* Rochester, Vt.: Destiny Books, 1995.

Lau, T. *The Handbook of Chinese Horoscopes.* London: Souvenir Press, 1979.

Madden, Kristin. *Pagan Parenting.* Niceville, Flor.: Spilled Candy, 2000.

——. *Pagan Homeschooling.* Niceville, Flor.: Spilled Candy, 2002.

McCoy Edain. *The Sabbats.* St. Paul, Minn.: Llewellyn Publications, 1999.

Melody. *Love is in the Earth: A Kaleidoscope of Crystals.* Richland, Wash.: EarthLove Publishing, 1991.

Parker, Janet, and Julie Stanton, ed. *Mythology, Myths, Legends, & Fantasies.* Australia: Global Book Publishing, 2003.

Peschel, Lisa. *A Practical Guide to The Runes.* St. Paul, Minn.: Llewellyn Publications, 1996.

Sutton, Maya Magee, Ph.D., and Nicholas Mann. *Druid Magic: The Practice of Celtic Wisdom.* St. Paul, Minn.: Llewellyn Publications, 2000.

Thorsson, Edred. *Futhark: A Handbook of Rune Magic.* York Beach, Maine: Samuel Weiser, Inc., 1984.

Wise, Tad. *Blessings on the Wind.* Vancouver: Chronicle Books, Raincoast Books, 2002.

Arts and Crafts

Gross, Gay Merrill. *Origami.* New York: Barnes & Noble Books, 2002.

Maguire, Mary. *Magic Lanterns.* Cincinnati, Ohio: Northern Light Books, 2002.

Painter, Lucy. *Get Crafty.* London: Joanna Lorenz, 1997.

Reader's Digest. *Crafts & Hobbies.* Pleasantville, N.Y.: Reader's Digest Association, Inc., 1979.

Robins, Deri, ed. *Step-by-step Crafts for Children.* New York: Kingfisher, 1996.

Summit, Ginger, and Jim Widess. *The Complete Book of Gourd Craft.* New York: Lark Books, 1996.

Sunset editorial staff with Robert and Joan Dawson. *Sculpture with Simple Materials.* Menlo Park, Calif.: Lane Books, 1966.

Mosaic

Fassett, Kaffe, and Candace Bahouth. *Mosaics.* London: Ebury Press, Random House, 2001.

Firth, Ann. *Pebble Mosaics.* Devon, England: David & Charles, Brunel House, 2002.

Fabric

Albrecht, Christian. *Batik.* London: Search Press, 1969.

Editors of Creative Publishing International, Inc. *Exploring Textile Arts.* Chanhassen, Minn.: Creative Publishing International, 2002.

Kanzinger, Linda S. *The Complete Book of Fabric Painting.* Portland: The Alcott Press, 1993.

McCormick Gordon, Maggi. *The Ultimate Sewing Book.* London: Collins & Brown, 2002.

Labyrinth

Attali, Jacques. *The Labyrinth in Culture and Society.* Berkeley, Calif.: North Atlantic Books, 1999.

West, Melissa Gayle. *Exploring the Labyrinth.* New York: Broadway Books, 2000.

Rubber Stamps

Mcgraw, MaryJo. *Creative Rubber Stamping Techniques.* Cincinnati: Northern Light Books, 1998.

Udell, Luann. *Rubber Stamp Carving.* New York: Lark Books, 2002.

Resources

Drum and Rattle Supplies

Centralia Fur & Hide
2012 Gallagher Road
Centralia, WA 98531
(877) 736–2525
www.furandhide.com
Layne@furandhide.com

Online Art Supplies

Axner Pottery Supply
clay and pottery supplies
www.axner.com

Dharma Trading
fabric dye and fabric art supplies
www.dharmatrading.com

Dick Blick
art materials
www.dickblick.com

The Leather Factory
leather and leather-craft supplies
www.leatherfactory.com

Organizations for Peace

Peace Education Foundation
(305) 576–5075/(800) 749–8838
www.peace-ed.org/
www.peaceeducation.com/

PeaceJam Foundation Headquarters
5605 Yukon Street
Arvada, CO 80002
(303) 455–2099
www.peacejam.org/index.html
info@peacejam.org

The World Peace Sanctuary
26 Benton Road
Wassaic, NY 12592
(845) 877–6093
www.worldpeace.org
info@worldpeace.org

Peace Pals Project
www.worldpeace.org/peacepals.html

Tolerance.org
c/o The Southern Poverty Law Center
400 Washington Avenue
Montgomery, AL 36104
(334) 956–8200
www.tolerance.org/

index

About the Authors

KRISTIN MADDEN (New Mexico) is a bestselling author of several books on paganism, shamanism, and parenting. She has had ongoing experience with Eastern and Western mystic paths since 1972 and is the Dean of Ardantane's School of Shamanic Studies. A Druid and tutor in the Order of Bards, Ovates, and Druids, Kristin is also a member of the Druid College of Healing.

LIZ ROBERTS (New Mexico) was born and raised in the south of England. She traveled extensively before settling in America. As a potter, Liz makes functional stoneware embellished with Celtic designs. Liz is a Peace Pals coordinator who works creatively with children of all ages to strengthen their connections to the Earth and expand their worldview so they might help create a more peaceful planet.